As a Christian woman, you want to glorify God and enjoy the abundant life that He has promised. However, fear, guilt, a poor self-image — perhaps even self-hatred — may be robbing you of experiencing the blessings of serenity and joy that He showers upon His children. In *The Confident Woman*, image improvement expert Joanne Wallace combines life-changing ideas with practical methods to show you how to get the most out of your life and your relationships.

You'll learn how to love and accept yourself, enhance your appearance, and enjoy your relationships with others. Joanne Wallace examines various passages of Scripture to assure you that as a woman created by God, it is His will that you develop both inner and outer beauty. You'll be encouraged by her warmth, candor, and keen insight and will become more vivacious and self-assured as you capture her enthusiasm and grace. This comprehensive, creative, and compassionate guide includes four pages of full-color illustrations, sketches, exercises, interesting self-tests, step-by-step directions, and more. *The Confident Woman* will enable you to improve every aspect of your life.

BY Joanne Wallace
The Image of Loveliness
Dress With Style
The Confident Woman

JOANNE WALLACE

The Confident Woman

Fleming H. Revell Company
Old Tappan, New Jersey

Library Of Congress Cataloging in Publication Data

Wallace, Joanne.
    The confident woman.

    Includes index.
    1. Women—Religious life.   2. Women—Life skills
guides.   I. Title.
BV4527.W34   1985   248.8′43   84-15122
ISBN 0-8007-1229-3

TO

Jim Wallace

my husband, who always believes in me.
Without him, it would be difficult
to be a confident woman.

Contents

Introduction   *11*

PART ONE: The Confident Woman Values Herself

1   What Makes a Confident Woman?   *17*
2   How to Have a Beautiful Personality   *23*
3   Seven Steps to Better Self-Esteem   *33*
Assignment   *39*

PART TWO: The Confident Woman Values Her Appearance

4   How to Create the Right Clothing Style   *45*
5   Body Messages   *69*
6   Exercise and Health for Your Well-Being   *93*
7   Face Facts   *109*
8   Hair Treatment   *119*
Assignment   *129*

PART THREE: The Confident Woman Values Her Relationships

9   Communication: Key to Confidence   *133*
10   Marriage, Sex, and a Beautiful You   *141*
11   Temptation: The Unmentionable Sin   *159*
12   Fear, Fantasy, and Guilt—Destroyers of Confidence   *165*
13   Forgiveness   *173*
Assignment   *177*
Closing Thoughts   *179*
Index   *181*

Acknowledgments

My special thanks to . . .

My daughter, Deanna Wallace Early, whose writing skills made this book possible!

Illustrator: Sherry LaMunyan

Photographers: Dean Early
Carole Day

Before/After Models: Tera Canant
Inez Costa
Karen Crook
Deanna Early
Leona Early
Sarah Okoye
Kathy Thomas
Debbie Threewit

Lounge Wear Models: Liz and Dawn Lundmark

Lounge Wear: *Intimique*, Lake Oswego, Oregon

Introduction

You have now taken one of the first steps toward becoming a confident woman. If you are reading this book, you have begun! Right now you can start becoming all that God intended you to be.

I used to be a woman who hated herself and her life. I was unhappy and looking for ways to escape myself. Today I love my life and myself. I have a new attitude and life-style.

What made the difference? Through a long process, I learned to trust myself. The American Heritage Dictionary defines *confidence* as "trust in a person or thing." To be a truly confident woman you must trust yourself.

In this book you'll read about many ways you can learn to trust yourself. Starting from the inside, you can become all that you were meant to be!

The first section of the book deals with your self-esteem and what it means to be a confident woman. Since I've been conducting my Image Improvement seminars in different churches across the United States and Canada, I have come to believe that the number one problem among women today is a lack of basic self-esteem. Here are just a few of the comments I heard during a recent seminar:

- I'm thirty-three years old and have been overweight for twenty-one years. I feel terribly ugly and I have never been able to lose this weight. Please pray that I may know what to do.

- Please pray that I can accept God's will for me as a woman. I presently feel like a dirty, useless object. I don't know what a lady or woman is to feel like. I am twenty years old and I'm beginning to see sex as the only way of having the intimate love I long to have.

- I'm scared and lonely. I wish I could love myself.

- I am lonely and sad. I am a senior citizen living alone and drinking too much wine. I am so lonely, I can't adjust. Help me, dear God.

These women are not alone. In my travels I hear from thousands of women who have exactly the same feelings and needs. We all need to be loved and accepted, but what we don't often realize is that this love and acceptance must come *first* from ourselves.

My three-year-old grandson, Aron, has a beautiful habit that I think all of us can adapt to our own situations. At night when he goes to bed he gives his daddy and mommy a big hug and kiss, but then he goes one step further. Before he gets into bed he wraps his arms around himself and gives himself a big squeeze. "I sure do like myself," he says.

Sometimes, you and I need to mentally or even physically hug ourselves. We need to be able to say, "I sure do like myself."

This attitude of really loving yourself begins from the inside but it also spills directly onto the outside. In the second section of the book, you will learn many ways to gain confidence in the way you look and dress. In most cases this is one of the easiest areas to improve. Once you feel good about yourself inside, the outside can be improved a great deal.

Physical attractiveness has a big impact on how you respond to yourself and others. In most cases, we all prefer a neat, attractive exterior. We may not want to admit it, but often our opinions of others are based on the way they look.

A University of Minnesota study shows that this preference for beauty starts early. Preschool children were found to be easily able to distinguish between attractive or unattractive people. The study also found that children, like adults, prefer being around attractive people.

Our appearance is also directly related to our self-image. When I feel a little blah or tired I find myself not really caring about what I wear, whether my hair is combed, or my makeup is applied correctly. I'm less able to respond positively to others, even my family.

However, when I've taken the time to improve my physical appearance I feel much more positive about all areas of my life.

Have you ever noticed that when you're feeling depressed you'll usually put on the drabbest thing in your closet—if you bother to get out of your bathrobe at all? On the other hand, if you're feeling terrific and looking forward to the day, you will dress in your favorite and most attractive outfit!

I believe that the inside of a person is by far the most important. Trying to improve the outer appearance alone is a waste of time, but this doesn't mean you should neglect the outside! Inner and outer beauty are very finely interwoven. It is hard to have one without the other.

Finally, when you have improved your self-esteem and outer attractiveness, you can begin to really work on your life-style. You will see changes in your marriage, family, and other relationships. You will begin to live up to your great potential.

In the third section of the book I share many ways you can improve your relationships; how to deal with guilt, fear, and fantasy; and how you can forgive yourself and others.

This may seem an impossible task. You may feel you have too far to go on the road to improving yourself. At one time, I felt exactly the same way, but it is never too late to begin. Whether you feel no confidence, some confidence, or a lot of confidence there is always room for growth.

Recently, I received a beautiful letter from a former student of the Image Improvement courses which helps to prove my point:

I want to share with you some of the positive things that have happened to me since I took your Image of Loveliness course.

I must say at first I was overwhelmed and thought it would be next to impossible to create this new image within me. I felt so lost. The revamping was more than I could undertake.

I wanted this "new me" so badly. I made up my mind to really concentrate and apply myself in all areas. It took time, but oh, it was worth it! After three years of thoroughly studying my Image notebook, recommended reading, and exercising, I can truly say I'm a better person inside and out. I feel good about myself. I'm still growing and learning!

Today is an exciting opportunity for you. Let's get started!

PART ONE

The Confident

Woman Values

Herself

Learn About:

- How to become confident from the inside out
- Comparing yourself with someone else
- Physical attractiveness vs. godliness
- How to develop your potential
- Loving yourself and others
- How to handle bad circumstances
- Being determined
- How to assert yourself
- Ways to enhance your self-esteem
- Becoming all God intends you to be

1

What Makes a Confident Woman?

One day when my three-year-old grandson, Aron, was visiting me, he began to recite people's names. He seemed to be thinking very hard and then said, "Daddy, Mommy, Grandpa, Grandma, Jesse, Erika, Brooke . . ." Puzzled, I interrupted him and asked, "Aron, what are you doing?" He looked astonished that I would even have to ask and proudly said, "I'm just listing all the people who like me!"

His response confirmed what I believe about human nature. We all need to be assured that we are loved and accepted. For others to like you, you've got to like yourself. It doesn't matter *who* you are, it does matter how you *feel* about yourself.

In Matthew 22:39, Jesus said, "Love your neighbor as you love yourself," (TEV). In Mark 12:31 it says, "You must love others as much as yourself." Why do you think you don't get along with others? Because you don't love and accept yourself.

Self-acceptance is the foundation for confidence. How you feel about yourself is directly related to how confident you are. Do you like yourself? Are you happy with who you are? Do you feel you have worth as a person? To be a confident woman, you should be able to answer yes to all three questions.

Throughout my growing-up years and into my mid-twenties, I couldn't answer yes to any of these questions. For some reason I felt I wasn't worth very much and I was filled with self-rejection. Because of this, I couldn't reach out to others. I found myself avoiding even my closest friends. I remember seeing a friend of mine in the grocery store and rather than say hello I turned around and walked out of the store!

17

I could not accept or love myself and consequently I could not love others. It came to the point where someone actually said to me, "Joanne, don't love me like you love yourself—I can't stand the hate!"

Finally, I had to come to the point where I was willing to change. This change occurred when God showed me through His Word, and through other people, how far I was from the woman He intended me to be. Slowly, I began to grow in self-acceptance and then confidence as I learned what tools are necessary for positive self-esteem. Eventually, I felt that the things I'd learned should be shared with other women like myself.

In 1969 I wrote and began teaching (in my home), the Image of Loveliness self-improvement course. This business/ministry rapidly outgrew its humble beginnings and my corporation, Image Improvement, Inc., now has franchised and certified teachers throughout the United States and in several foreign countries.

My personal ministry has also expanded, and I now travel every week, giving weekend seminars for different churches.

Through my travels and seminars, I've found there are basic areas that need to be dealt with in accepting yourself.

Comparison

The first problem is comparison. You need to realize that God has a special place for you. You are unique, and God wants to use you in a way different from anyone else.

You may have times when you feel inferior to someone else, or maybe even superior. Both attitudes are wrong. Comparison is extremely damaging; it brings depression and is a tool used by Satan, not God. You need to see the good in other people and learn from them, but you should not allow yourself to be envious or jealous in your comparison. Compete only against yourself. Urge yourself to do a better job or handle a relationship better than you did the last time.

At one point in my life I was constantly comparing myself with a woman I knew. I thought she was so perfect and had everything going her way. Finally, I just came out and told her about my feelings of inferiority. To my amazement I found out that this woman had been feeling inferior to me! We had both been looking at each other through the eyes of comparison, and it had blinded us to the true perspective.

Years ago I used to watch Colleen Townsend Evans in the Billy Graham movies. I'd dream about what it would be like to actually meet her. She was a kind of role model for me.

Not too long ago, I received a phone call asking me to speak at a large church in Phoenix. There were other keynote speakers besides myself and one of them was Colleen Townsend Evans. I was so excited and couldn't wait to meet her!

About two weeks before I was to speak I began to get frightened. I started to compare myself with Colleen and decided I didn't quite measure up. For the next two weeks I assailed myself with thoughts like, *Who would want to hear me speak when Colleen Townsend Evans is there?* and *How can I ever share a platform with someone like her?*

It got so bad that the day before I was to speak I seriously thought of calling to tell them I couldn't make it because I was sick! Actually, I *was* sick—sick to my stomach with worry and self-doubts.

Then I remembered that I shouldn't say no to something as a result of comparing myself with someone else. I should just go and do my best.

That weekend was one of the most marvelous weekends of my life. Colleen Townsend Evans was everything I thought she'd be. Her life and her message enriched me with a spiritual blessing, and meeting her was a dream come true!

If I'd said no and cancelled out, I would have really missed out on God's wonderful plan for my life. Don't let yourself say no to things because you feel you won't measure up to someone else.

Galatians 6:4, 5 says, "Let everyone be sure that he is doing his very best, for then he will have the personal satisfaction of work well done, and won't need to compare himself with someone else. Each of us must bear some faults and burdens of his own. For none of us is perfect!"

Don't Put Yourself Down

Maybe you feel your "imperfections" more acutely than others. If so, you may need to work on the next area, which is not putting yourself down. As Robert Schuller says, "No one puts God's people down more than themselves."

Putting yourself down not only hurts your performance but also your relationships with others and eventually your walk with God. It is too easy to say, "I'm so dumb," "I'm so clumsy," "I'm so stupid." When you knock yourself it is just like saying, "God, when you made me you did a lousy job." Nothing could be further from the truth. When God made you He did an absolutely marvelous job! He knew what He was doing.

Psalms 139:13, 14 says, "You made all the delicate, inner parts of my body, and knit them together in my mother's womb. Thank you for making me so wonderfully complex! It is amazing to think about. Your workmanship is marvelous—and how well I know it."

God knew you and formed you in your mother's womb. God made you wonderfully complex. It's important to see yourself as God sees you. God made you as a mental, spiritual, and *physical* being. Part of seeing yourself from God's point of view means accepting your body.

Is Physical Beauty Okay?

At one time I was frightened of beauty—physical beauty—because I thought it was "unchristian." I had always heard that as a Christian I should not concern myself with my outer appearance. I thought women who were physically attractive could not possibly have much spiritual depth.

I now know how wrong I was. I've been working with women for over fifteen years and I've learned that physical attractiveness greatly influences the self-image. If you are to love your neighbor as you love yourself, you've also got to love the way you look. How you look is closely related to how you feel about yourself. Sometimes it is hard to know which comes first. Does your physical attractiveness improve your self-image, or does your self-image improve your physical attractiveness? Either way, your outer appearance is extremely important in telling others how you feel about yourself.

If you are hesitant about the fact that being godly and being beautiful are compatible ideas, let's look at some of the women in the Bible. It is interesting to note that many of the women God significantly used were physically very beautiful.

Of course, the very first woman was Eve. I know that she must have been the most beautiful and magnificent woman ever created. After all, she was perfect and without sin and God said, "It is good." Adam was also excited about her because it says in Genesis 2:23 that when Adam saw her he exclaimed, "This is it!"

What about Sarah, Abraham's wife? She was so beautiful that when Abraham went to live in Egypt he told Sarah to tell everyone she was his sister. He was frightened that if people knew she was his wife someone would kill him to get to her. Genesis 12:14 says, "And sure enough, when they arrived in Egypt everyone spoke of her beauty."

Rebekah was another example of a godly woman who was also physically beautiful. Genesis 24:16 (KJV) says Rebekah was ". . . very fair to look upon."

Jacob's wife Rachel was also very beautiful. Genesis 29:17 describes Rachel this way: ". . . Rachel was shapely, and in every way a beauty." In fact, Jacob worked fourteen years for Rachel's father in order to be allowed to marry Rachel.

My favorite Bible beauty is Esther. She is what I would call the "beauty queen" of the Bible. If there were self-improvement courses available when Esther was alive, I'm sure she took them! She spent one whole year of her life trying all kinds of perfumes, ointments, and fabrics to make herself as beautiful as possible. Although this sounds frivolous, it enabled her to become queen of her land and eventually, she was responsible for saving the Jewish population of her time from extinction.

Esther's beauty was not a vain beauty. It was a beauty dedicated and given to God, completely and totally. It was beauty that began from within and spilled over onto the outside.

This is the type of beauty that I advocate. When you can honor God with your appearance, you don't have to worry about a thing called pride. If you give your physical appearance to God, you won't find yourself checking the mirror every five minutes to see how you look.

In dealing with this matter of physical beauty, it is important to understand the true context of 1 Peter 3:3, 4 which says, "Your beauty should not be dependent upon an elaborate coiffure, or on the wearing of jewellery or fine clothes, but on the inner personality—the unfading loveliness of a calm and gentle spirit, a thing very precious in the eyes of God'' (PHILLIPS).

The key word here is *dependent*. Your beauty should not be *dependent* on outer adornment, but outer adornment is not wrong in itself. It is my understanding that when Peter wrote his letter, the women of his age were spending hours a day on their outer appearance. They were exclusively concerned with how they looked, and so Peter sent the warning that they should not be dependent on outer beauty; in other words, it should not come first in their lives.

When outer beauty comes first in your life, it is hollow and displeasing to God, but a beauty that begins from within should most definitely influence your outer appearance. As a representative of Christ, your appearance should be as attractive as possible so that others will be drawn to you.

What draws others to you in the first place is often your appearance. God has given us eyesight, and we tend to judge others primarily on visual images when we first meet. Others may never get to know what a wonderful personality you have if you don't look interesting enough to pursue. If they don't get to know you, they may never get to know Christ through you. When you don't take care of your appearance, you are nonverbally telling others, "I'm not worth it." They pick up on this message and take you at your word!

I will cover specific ways to improve your outer appearance in part 2 because I think it is important for you to look your very best to honor God. It is also important to look good for your family's sake. I know my husband responds more positively to me when I've taken the time to fix my hair and put on some makeup. I love my husband and I want to look my best for him.

In my travels I've seldom met a woman who is completely satisfied with herself. Most people have some area in their lives and appearance they would like to change.

You may not be the most beautiful woman in the world, but you can be the most attractive "you" there is. It may take a little effort, but there is potential in every single one of us.

If you could change your appearance, how would you want to look? Dr. Robert Kotler,* a plastic surgeon, has found that many of his patients want their faces to resemble celebrities. In his work he finds that the greatest number of women patients ask for the following characteristics:

Lower lip—like that of Brooke Shields
Eyes—Crystal Gayle
Upper Lip (Cupid's bow)—Barbi Benton
Chin—Jaclyn Smith
Ears—Bo Derek
Cheekbones—Jane Fonda
Forehead—Farrah Fawcett
Nose—Dolly Parton

According to Dr. Kotler, many people would like to change their appearance. Although plastic surgery may not be the answer for all, I do know it is important to be satisfied with the way you look.

* Dr. Kotler is president of the American Nasal and Facial Surgery Institute, Inc.

In improving your appearance you've got to do two things: Change the things you can and accept the things you can't change. Most of us would like to improve our appearance in some way. In this book you will discover many ways to improve your appearance through clothing, hairstyle, makeup, exercise, and body language. You have the power to effect change in these areas. However, there may be some things about your appearance you can never change.

When I was in seventh grade, I was 5 feet 7 inches tall and wore size 9 shoes. I just knew that if I were 5 feet 2 inches tall and wore size 6 shoes, people would like me better. I constantly worried about something I had no control over. It made me envious of the other girls, and I started feeling inferior to them. I was miserable and my misery was useless! I didn't shrink one inch!

Today I am 5 feet 8½ and wear size 10 shoes. I can either accept this or make myself miserable about being a tall woman with big feet!

My sister, Jean Gildersleeve, is a junior high school counselor. She comes in contact with many teenagers who are having trouble with their self-image. She offers this advice which applies to all of us:

> Part of being human is having problems and hang-ups. We often feel we need to fix or change ourselves to conform to some more perfect example of humanity.
>
> We can spend a lot of time and negative thought trying to change things that we should accept. We pray that God will use us in spite of our imperfections. This I feel is negative thinking and self-rejection. We need to pray, "God use me *because* of the kind of person I am." God made us and allowed us to have certain experiences and grow up in particular circumstances. This, along with the genetic factor, makes us who we are.
>
> Let's go beyond accepting the things we cannot change. Let's *use* the things we cannot change.

Do you believe God can *use* the things you cannot change? I know He can!

You may feel unattractive because of something you cannot change. It may be your height, the size of your nose, or any number of things. Whatever it is, you've got to learn to accept it. If there is absolutely nothing you can do about it, come to terms with it. Don't let it interfere with how you feel about yourself and especially don't let it interfere with God's plans for you.

God loves you just the way you are. God loves even the things you cannot change. He loves YOU—imperfections and all. He wants to use you and flow through you to others. You need to see yourself from God's point of view. You are beautiful and because of this you can have confidence. Your ultimate worth as a person is based on that which is eternal—GOD. Knowing this, believing this, will result in the assurance that you are loved and accepted as you are. I can think of no better basis for living life with confidence.

2

How to Have

a Beautiful

Personality

Last Christmas my daughter, Deanna, received a beautiful lamp that her husband, Dean, had made for her. When she unwrapped it, we all gasped. It looked absolutely perfect. It was very carefully hand fashioned and the workmanship was excellent.

However, something was missing. Even though the lamp was beautiful, it was not living up to its potential. Without a vital connection it would never fulfill its purpose. Someone had to plug it in and turn on the switch.

You are like that lamp. You are hand fashioned by God and the workmanship is excellent. In fact, you have all the parts necessary to bring light to yourself and to the world. You just need that vital connection. Someone has to turn on the switch!

That vital connection is a personal relationship with Jesus Christ. It's important to realize that He is waiting to "turn on the switch" so that you can fulfill your great potential.

In developing your potential I can think of no better place to start than your personality. The most common question I hear from the women I meet is, "How can I have a more attractive personality?"

This is a valid question as your personality is an important expression of who you are and although your personality is unique, there are still qualities you can possess that will draw others to you.

The secret is to develop Christlike qualities in your life. If you have accepted Christ as your Savior, He wants to live His life in and through you. However, this does not mean that you no longer have problems or sin in your life. Allowing Christ to flow through you is a daily or an hourly process of *consent*. It is *your choice*. You can allow Christ's qualities to be evident or you can continue in your own way.

Remember, your consent is necessary if you desire Christlike qualities in your life. Galatians 5:22, 23 tells us what these qualities are: "But when the Holy Spirit controls our lives he will produce this kind of fruit in us: love, joy, peace, patience, kindness, goodness, faithfulness, gentleness and self-control; and here there is no conflict with Jewish laws."

As a Christian woman, the fruits of the Spirit should be evident in your life and personality. Although all of the fruits are important, let's look at how some of them can be displayed in your personality.

The Greatest Quality

The greatest of these qualities is love. It is really the primary characteristic. First Corinthians 14:1 says, "Let love be your greatest aim . . . ," 1 Corinthians 16:14 says, "and whatever you do, do it with kindness and love," and 1 John 4:16, 17 says, "God is love, and anyone who lives in love is living with God and God is living in him. And as we live with Christ our love grows more perfect. . . ."

Love has the power to change the course of a life. I have seen the dramatic power of love in my own family. On August 13, 1983, I became a grandmother for the second time; only this time my granddaughter came to our family from the other side of the world. Deanna and Dean adopted a little girl from Korea. Her name is Kimberly Joanne and she is such a joy to our family.

However, when Kimberly first arrived in America at two and a half years of age, she had only been walking for about three months, weighed less than twenty pounds, and did not know how to kiss or hug anyone. She had lived most of her life in an orphanage and was moved around to several different foster homes. She suffered from lack of love and lack of stimulation.

Within three days of living in her new permanent home, her favorite thing to do was hug and kiss. Her first English sentence was, "I love you." She has gained several pounds, has grown taller, and can now run on legs that barely supported her before.

She is a living example of the power of love. Before she knew love, she was struggling to survive. Her development was extremely delayed and her future was uncertain. Today, because of love, she is growing and changing by leaps and bounds. Her future is limitless and she has the opportunity to become all God intends her to be.

We all need love to survive. Why is it that the thing we need most we resist? Why is it often so hard to say, "I love you"? Love is the most powerful force in our world today; we need to be channeling that force to other people.

A woman I know was separated from her husband and it looked as though a divorce was coming. They had been having many problems and had tried several reconciliations to no avail.

When this woman heard me speak, I told of the importance of telling others verbally that we love them. She discussed this with her husband and they decided they would try one more time to stay together. This time, however, there was to be an important difference. They were going to say, "I love you," to each other at least three times a day—and mean it. They would not do it out of duty or say it carelessly, they would say it and live it.

Two years later she has written to tell me that they are still together and not once have they forgotten their promise. She believes it is an important reason they are still together.

One of my Image Improvement teachers, Cindy Smith of Fort Morgan, Colorado, wrote me this letter:

> I had a student who attended my first eight-week session. I could sense she was right on the edge of some exciting changes in her life.
>
> Her mother also desired to take the classes and when the next eight-week session began I had the privilege of meeting her. As always, during the introductory class, we discussed giving and receiving love, compliments, nonverbal communication, and many other things.
>
> Shortly after the class, both mother and daughter were together and began sharing with each other. The mother looked at her daughter and said, "I'm really proud of you." The daughter turned to her mother with tears in her eyes and said, "I've waited a long time to hear you say that."
>
> They had experienced a few rocky years in their relationship with each other and have now begun a fairly good relationship again.

Who do you need to say "I love you" to today? _____

Please do it. Don't let another day go by without saying these vital words.

The Compatible Qualities

In Galatians 5:22 you may notice that Paul lists joy and peace as following love. This is true in the literal sense as well. When you begin to really love others, joy and peace follow.

John 15:11 says, "I have told you this so that you will be filled with my joy. Yes, your cup of joy will overflow!" Nehemiah 8:10 says, ". . . for the joy of the Lord is your strength. . . ."

What is your definition of *joy?* Mine is **J**esus **O**verflowing **Y**ou. Write down how you would describe joy using these three letters:

J _____

O _____

Y _____

Joy literally means a sense of fulfillment that is not based on circumstances. It should not be mistaken for happiness. Happiness is based on circumstances, joy is based on your relationship with God.

You can have a sense of fulfillment even in the midst of bad circumstances.

However, if your joy is based on circumstances it will never last. Ultimately, all people and all things will disappoint you.

Jesus was betrayed by every single one of His disciples. If He had been dependent upon them for His fulfillment He would have been destroyed. Instead, His strength and fulfillment came from His Heavenly Father and He was able to triumph over the worst of circumstances.

I knew a woman who exemplified this Christlike attitude. She always seemed to be on top of the world. It seemed that everything went her way. When I looked at this woman I thought she didn't have a care in the world. Her cheerfulness was contagious, and it seemed she was never without a heart-warming smile. She exuded joy in everything she did.

Later I found out that this beautiful woman had cancer. She lived with excruciating pain and the knowledge of certain death. Eventually she did die, but never once did I see even so much as a frown upon her face.

Her circumstances would be the envy of no one, yet her spirit bubbled with joy. She had learned the secret of depending on God for her fulfillment.

Joy is evident when you learn that, despite your circumstances, God is in control.

When you know that God is in control, another immediate benefit is a deep feeling of peace. Like joy, real peace is based on your relationship with God instead of your circumstances.

Colossians 3:15 says, "Let the peace of heart which comes from Christ be always present in your hearts and lives, for this is your responsibility and privilege as members of his body. . . ."

Peace of mind is your responsibility and your privilege. Jesus describes this peace by saying, "I am leaving you with a gift—peace of mind and heart! And the peace I give isn't fragile like the peace the world gives. So don't be troubled or afraid" (John 14:27).

Henry Drummond tells the story about two artists who were commissioned to paint their versions of what peace looked like.

The first artist painted a serene landscape with rolling hills and a smooth glasslike lake. A perfect tranquility permeated the scene. This type of peace is often the only peace many people ever know.

The second artist painted a stormy scene with a huge waterfall crashing down on high, jagged cliffs. Amidst this turbulence, the artist painted a tall, slender birch tree with its branches reaching just over the foaming water. Tucked in a branch of this tree was a bird's nest. Inside the nest was a small bird fast asleep.

What an example of true peace. Even amid the crashing, thundering torrent of our daily struggles, we can rest easy knowing that God is in control.

John 16:33 says, "I have told you this so that you will have peace of heart and mind. Here on earth you will have many trials and sorrows; but cheer up, for I have overcome the world."

When my grandson goes to bed at night, he cannot sleep unless he knows his daddy will be watching over him. Because his daddy always comes to him when he calls in the night, Aron believes his daddy stays up all night to protect him. He doesn't realize yet that his daddy has to sleep too.

Our Father in heaven is also watching out for us. Peace can be ours when we realize God is always there waiting for us, and He never sleeps!

Are you feeling anxious or worried over something in your life? Write down what it is: _____

_____

_____

Right now ask God to give you peace about this situation. Remember, you must give Him *consent* to flood your soul with peace.

Fear and peace are incompatible. Second Timothy 1:7 says, "For God hath not given us the spirit of fear; but of power, and of love, and of a sound mind" (KJV).

Unfortunately, we all have fears. The number one universal fear is the fear of speaking in front of an audience. I know about this fear firsthand. Not too long ago I was giving a "Success Dress" seminar for 500 women in a large corporation.

Before I spoke I asked for a neck microphone so that my hands would be free to work with the pieces of clothing I was showing. When I got to the seminar a neck microphone wasn't available. The only microphone in the building was a big, heavy monster with a long, thick cord. I had no choice, so I improvised. With a long strip of cloth I tied this heavy microphone around my neck. It was uncomfortable, and the cord weighed it down even more. As I began, I breathed a silent prayer, *Oh, Lord, please let me forget about this heavy cord.*

I'm living proof that God answers prayer. I forgot all about the bulky microphone and cord. In fact, I forgot so completely that in the middle of my presentation the cord got wrapped around my feet and when I moved I fell flat on my face. I didn't just trip—I *fell* in front of 500 women!

Of course, the women all started laughing, and I thought they'd never stop. It was so embarrassing that I yelled, "Five-minute break!" and this made them laugh even louder.

I finally got untangled from the cord and made my way to the back of the room. My husband had accompanied me to the seminar, and as I went toward him he said, "You were great! You remembered to do something very important!"

I thought he must be going crazy, but I went along with him and asked, "Oh, really? What?" Then Jim capped off my whole day by saying, "Well, when you fell you remembered to keep your knees together!"

After that experience I could have let embarrassment and fear take over. I could have said I would never speak in front of an audience again. But, you see, it isn't important how many times we fall in life—we do it often—it is important how many times we pick ourselves up and keep going.

Jeremiah 8:4 says, ". . . When a person falls, he jumps up again. . . ." You and I must force ourselves to do the things we are afraid to do. This means never giving up.

Qualities That Never Give Up

Patience is a quality that never gives up. For everyday living this means *determination*. There are a lot of quitters in the world—too many. It is easy not to try—or to try once and then never try again.

Your patient determination will assure you of success in life. First Corinthians 15:58 says, ". . . since future victory is sure, be strong and steady, always abounding in the Lord's work, for you know that nothing you do for the Lord is ever wasted. . . ."

Cheryl Prewitt Blackwood, Miss America 1980 and a beautiful Christian woman, knows about this patient determination. She entered many pageants before she finally won the title of Miss America. She lost many times but was determined to keep trying.

The first year she competed in her local pageant she was voted first runner-up. The second year she tried, she was voted second runner-up. The third year she tried again and was voted third runner-up. Now what do you think you would do? It was quite embarrassing, but she knew that someway, somehow, God would use her, and she was willing to try again. The next year she went on to win her local and state titles and finally the Miss America pageant.

Being determined means setting goals and sticking to them. It means being patient enough to wait, but also courageous enough to stick it out until the end.

My daughter has a good friend, Randy McMillan, who is blind. He became blind shortly after birth and so cannot remember ever having sight.

As Randy grew up he had two choices. He could either make excuses for his blindness and feel sorry for himself, or he could accept himself and go on from there. Fortunately, he chose the latter.

As a child, Randy loved his radio. Because of his radio he learned to love music and sports. These two interests led him to set goals for himself.

Like a lot of children, he took piano lessons. Unlike a lot of children, he stuck with it. Without the aid of written music, he is now one of the finest pianists I've ever heard.

He also loved sports. Being blind, participating in sports wasn't very feasible. That didn't stop him though. He just pursued his interest in sports through a different channel.

Today he is a sportscaster for a radio station in Seattle, Washington. Although he cannot do play-by-play action reporting, he attends all the important sporting events and reports the sports news during regular broadcasts.

Randy McMillan is determined. He knows how to set goals and stick with them. He is making the most of his interests and talents.

It is so important that you have that kind of determination. Isaiah 50:7 says, "Because the Lord God helps me, I will not be dismayed; therefore, I have set my face like flint to do his will, and I know that I will triumph." You will never triumph in life unless you are determined. You may never know what God has in store for you unless you keep trying.

What goal do you have for yourself? _____

_____

_____

If it is a worthwhile goal, have patience and be determined that it will happen. Memorize 2 Corinthians 4:8, 9 which says, "We are pressed on every side by troubles, but not crushed and broken. We are perplexed because we don't know why things happen as they do, but we don't give up and quit. . . . We get knocked down, but we get up again and keep going."

This determination also has another side to it. It can lead to assertiveness. This assertiveness is not aggressiveness. Aggressiveness is an attitude that comes out of fear, assertiveness is an attitude that comes out of confidence.

I firmly believe that Christian women should assert themselves in a loving way. I have been praying about this in my own life because I grew up thinking I should be sweet, loving, and everybody's doormat. I used to think that being patient meant letting everyone walk all over me. Since then, I've learned that it is better to be honest and have the courage of my convictions. Ephesians 4:15 (KJV) says, "But speaking the truth in love . . ." and Colossians 3:17 says, "Whatever you do or say, let it be as a representative of the Lord Jesus. . . ."

Representing Jesus Christ gives you the authority to speak your mind, but representing Christ also means that you represent *love*. I know it is important for us to be loving, this should be foremost in all our dealings with others, but I'm not convinced that anyone should walk all over us.

What an exciting day it was when my television show was accepted by Christian Broadcasting Network (CBN) to be aired on a national basis. I knew that this was an answer to prayer. But, I had also been praying that God would show me His direction for my show. The network wanted a daily show, and I was worried about the time element; so I had turned the whole thing over to God.

Two weeks before the programs were to begin airing, I received a telephone call saying that there had been a change at the network and my show was going to be cancelled. I don't like the word *cancelled*. The network was going to put a two-hour Christian movie in my show's place.

At that point, all my Christian upbringing told me to be sweetly demure and give up without a fight. After all, women are not supposed to be assertive, right? Well, as all those thoughts were running through my head, I prayed for a boldness that I had never had before. I really believe it was of the Lord when I found myself saying to the network executive, "First off, I want you to know that I have totally given this show to the Lord and I want what He wants. Second, I think your decision not to air the show is very sad because it is the only program like it (helping women feel good and look good too) on Christian television. I really think it would be a tragedy to miss it. And third, Jesus Christ is my Source and because of this I am not a quitter. You will hear from me again sometime."

The executive listened carefully and said he would continue to pray about it.

After I hung up I was filled with such a peace in my soul and I could say, "Thank You, Lord," in a situation where I might otherwise have felt like crying.

I called my husband and told him the show was going to be cancelled and he said, "Praise the Lord!" I said, "*What?*" and he said, "Praise the Lord because now you know this is the answer." We talked of the peace we both felt and our assurance that God was in control.

That afternoon I had extra phone calls to make and I was on the phone for about two hours. As soon as I finished my calls the phone rang. It was the network. The executive said, "What have you been doing? I've been trying to reach you for hours. I couldn't stop thinking about what you said, and we've decided that we are not going to cancel the show. We're going to put it on Sunday afternoons and it will be in a once-a-week time slot."

It was exactly what I'd wanted all along! I believe that God had to take it away in order to find out exactly what my priorities were.

God never allows anything into our lives, I believe, but what we can handle. And when He takes something away, He will always replace it with something as good or better.

I also learned something else from that incident. I learned that assertiveness can be a good thing. Without it I would probably not have gotten a second chance.

Last month I boarded an airplane and went to my seat assignment in the no-smoking section. Once the plane was in the air, the businessman beside me lit up a cigarette. Instead of remaining quiet, I kindly, but assertively, said, "Sir, you are seated in the no-smoking section." He looked at me unhappily and said, "Are you complaining?" Firmly, but without any anger, I said, "Yes, I am, and if you do not put out your cigarette I am going to call the stewardess." He quickly put out his cigarette.

Although I thought I'd probably ended any other communication with him, later on, we actually began a pleasant conversation. He seemed to listen attentively and show respect for me in a way I found refreshing.

Again, I learned that loving assertiveness—which is not aggression—can be a valuable character quality.

On a scale of 1 to 10 how determined do you think you are? _____

How assertive? _____

In your own words, write the difference between being assertive and being

aggressive: _____

_____

_____

_____

Practice loving assertiveness. Speak the truth in love. Let Christ's power flow through you and give Him your consent for His control.

The Necessary Quality

Practicing a loving, patient determination requires a good dose of self-control. This self-control is really discipline and if you're like me, discipline is the most difficult of all the character qualities.

Discipline is needed in our bodies, our sexuality, our appetite for food, and so many things! Sometimes, this self-control may seem impossible. In times like these, it is important to remember that Jesus Christ was tempted in all ways and He resisted temptation through self-control. Matthew 4:1–11 tells the story about Christ's temptation. Reading this story makes one thing clear: Jesus Christ had discipline.

With Jesus Christ in control, discipline should be evident in your life as well. Second Timothy 2:1 says, "Be strong with the strength Christ Jesus gives you." Self-control really means God's control. If you have discipline, you won't be a slave to every whim and fancy that comes along. You will be free to accomplish your goals.

Part of my struggle as a person is learning to yield to God's Spirit in this matter of discipline. I'm so glad that God allows things in our lives so that we can be drawn to Him.

God is dealing with me in the matter of disciplining my emotions. One example of this stands out in my mind.

It happened when my daughter and I decided we would take our annual trip to Seaside, Oregon, to attend the Miss Oregon pageant. Deanna competed in the pageant one year, so every year after we've tried to attend. It is our special weekend together.

This particular time I was speaking in Seattle, Washington, the day of the pageant and I was in a rush to get home. Deanna had had a full day as well, and we were both a little grumpy as we threw everything into the car. We had just enough time to make the two-and-a-half-hour drive to Seaside and get there for the pageant.

On the way there we practically broke the speed limit and we arrived in Seaside just as the pageant was supposed to begin.

As we drove into that small city I said, "Where are all the people? There are hardly any cars here!" And Deanna said, "Mom, I guess we're late so we'd better hurry and get to the Convention Center."

When we got to the Convention Center, there were no cars or people there either. We drove around to the back to look for a new parking lot or some explanation of what was happening. As we drove back to the front I looked at the huge marquee and it said Flea Market This Weekend.

Deanna and I still didn't know what was wrong so we decided to drive over to the high school where they had held the pageant many years before. On our way to the high school, a horrible thought struck me. I pulled over to the curb and said, "Deanna, I'd better check my tickets."

The tickets confirmed my worst fear—the pageant was scheduled for the next weekend! I started to get all upset, and Deanna started to laugh. (She has a great sense of humor—she gets it from her dad!) She laughed as if she had gone crazy. She slapped her leg and said, "I love it, I love it, I love it! It's the best day of my life!"

I said, "Are you crazy? What are you talking about?" and she replied, "Mom, I love it because you can't do a thing about it!"

At this point I was ready to explode. My daughter knows that I am a very organized person. In fact, I like to organize organization. Sometimes, it is difficult for me to allow for humanness in myself and others.

But, I had two options. I could explode or I could yield to the Spirit of God. I decided to laugh with Deanna as I silently prayed, *Okay, Lord, I don't understand this. You know I have work to do at the office and I can't really waste my time on wild goose chases, but I thank You that You know what You're doing.*

Deanna and I had the best weekend we had had together in a long time. We needed that weekend without having business or anything else to do.

God did know what He was doing. I guess He doesn't need me to be the greatest organizer in the world. All He wants me to do is to yield myself completely to Him. My self-control is really *His control.*

Where in your life do you need more self-control? _____

_____

_____

_____

When you feel your control slipping, ask God to take over. Relax and let Him work in this area of discipline. Don't fear His control. First John 4:18 says, "We need have no fear of someone who loves us perfectly; his perfect love for us eliminates all dread of what he might do to us. . . ."

God intends for you to have a beautiful personality. Begin to develop love, joy, peace, patient determination, loving assertiveness, and self-control today. Before you act, stop, think, then submit to God and let His Spirit bear fruit in your life. If you do this, your personality will sparkle with qualities guaranteed to draw others to you.

Developing these qualities may not always be easy. In your life you will have many mountains and valleys to cross. Just remember that fruit grows in the valleys, not the mountains!

My prayer for you is that Psalms 1:3 will describe your life: "They are like trees along a river bank bearing luscious fruit each season without fail. Their leaves shall never wither, and all they do shall prosper."

3

Seven Steps
to Better
Self-Esteem

A little girl was studying a map of the United States. Her mother was nearby, and the little girl asked, "Mommy, why are all the rivers crooked?"

Her mother replied, "Because, honey, they follow the path of least resistance." In other words, rivers take the easy route.

Sometimes we are guilty of this same maneuver. Often, we take the path of least resistance. It is easier to "go with the flow," and so our lives become crooked and our self-images become warped.

It is interesting to note that there are two possible attitudes toward self that emerge from the Scriptures.

The first attitude is selfishness. It is shown in a person who loves herself with a greedy love that is insatiable. It is a love that would be better termed lust. A selfish person lusts after self-glory. Needless to say, selfishness is a sin.

The second attitude is a healthy self-love. It is not arrogance. It is a love that values God's creation—you. It is a love that begins with self but doesn't stop there, it is just the beginning of a love that encompasses everyone. This is love that God intended you to have.

When you understand your own worth as a person you can then forget about yourself and concentrate on others. When you come to the point of accepting yourself, you can then forget yourself and God can really use you.

One of my Image Improvement teachers, Rhonda Lynn from Bethlehem, Pennsylvania, recently sent me a letter she received from one of her students. Here is part of what her student had to say:

> . . . how wonderful life is when I am able to forget about myself and think of others first. It isn't easy, but just trying makes a difference. I've discovered that if I start

good feelings and good deeds toward others first, these feelings and deeds snow-ball and return to me. Now I try my hardest to think about others first and you know what, by doing that my self-esteem has risen immensely. It feels great not worrying about what others think of me. I'm not as afraid to open up to others and a lot of my feelings of jealousy, envy, and anger are slowly going away.

This woman is learning some of the exciting benefits of self-acceptance. She is discovering the whole point of living. You see, the foundation for your self-worth is based upon that which is eternal—*God*. Second Corinthians 3:5 (NAS) says, "Not that we are adequate in ourselves to consider anything as coming from ourselves, but our adequacy is from God." Instead of looking to men for adequacy, as the world does, you are to look to God, who is your total, complete, and supreme adequacy.

You may need some help to get back on the right course. There are seven basic steps that you can take to improve your life and your self-esteem.

1. Associate With Positive People

The first step to better self-esteem is to surround yourself with positive people. Be with people who lift you up and make you feel good.

If you find yourself with negative people, their attitude will rub off on you. The same is also true of surrounding yourself with positive people.

I had an experience with this when I was in my dentist's office. I was waiting to have my teeth cleaned when a friend of mine walked into the office. She was also waiting for an appointment and she sat down next to me.

I was very excited that day because I was going to the Oregon State Fair later in the evening. I asked her if she was going to the fair and her answer is still ringing in my ears: "Are you kidding? I wouldn't be caught dead there. I hate the way the mothers are always yelling at their naughty kids, the kids always have dirty faces, the place is full of pushing, shoving crowds, stinky live-stock, and carnival rides that make me sick."

Believe me, my enthusiasm for the fair was dampened after her tirade. How-ever, I realized that I saw the fair differently. I saw it as a fun place to go with a variety of exciting things to see and do. I went anyway and had a great time.

My poor friend, however, stayed home. She was burdened with a negative attitude. It has added years to her appearance and the lines in her face are etched with bitterness.

It is easy to find negative people. They are always waiting to rain on your parade. When I decided to try for the Mrs. Oregon title (finalist in Mrs. America pageant) I had some friends who said, "Oh, Joanne, if you are in that pageant you will lose your Christianity." They even had special prayer meetings for me!

I went ahead with the pageant and won. Guess what? I'm still a Christian; and because of the opportunities I was given as Mrs. Oregon, I was able to share about Jesus Christ with people I would not otherwise have met.

Negative *people* can be deadly. Negative *thinking* is certain death.

To understand this, let's pretend that you're at home, preparing a cup of coffee. You've just filled the cup and you are waiting for it to cool. You go into another room to get dressed and while you're gone someone comes in and drops cyanide into the cup.

It doesn't matter who puts the cyanide in the coffee. It could be your best friend or a perfect stranger. But, if you drink the coffee only one thing will happen: You will die.

Negative people are like that. They drop poison into your life. It doesn't matter who they are, but if you allow their poison into your system, your healthy self-image will die.

Try to surround yourself with positive people. If this is not possible, do not allow negative thoughts to creep into your life. If you notice this happening, immediately turn it over to God and ask Him for a fresh, positive outlook. Remember, God is a *positive* God.

2. Find a Good Sounding Board

The second step toward healthy self-esteem is to share your frustrations of self-acceptance with someone else. It may be your husband or your best friend. It may be your next-door neighbor or someone in your church. Whoever it is, it's important to share your frustration with others. You will probably be surprised at how the problem of low self-esteem is shared universally. No one is immune to nagging self-doubt. That is why it is important to share our doubts. We can then learn from another's mistakes and help one another with this problem.

My son, Bob, had a problem with his self-image when he was in junior high school. His dad was the coach of his school and naturally the other students expected Bob to participate in sports.

Bob was not really interested in competitive athletics and as a consequence he was teased by the other kids. They called him a sissy, which is a terrible thing for a junior high boy to hear.

For a long time, Bob did not tell me about what was going on at school. He kept it inside and his self-image really suffered. I knew something was wrong, but I was powerless to help.

Finally, Bob shared with me what was happening. It was such a relief to him to have that burden off his mind, that I immediately noticed a positive change.

Not long after that, he came to me all excited because he'd figured out another way to be involved in school. He would try to run for class president.

He began to have a healthy respect for himself, and in his senior year of high school he was the student body president and was voted "Boy of the Year" by the students.

It all began when he was willing to share his problem and then was free to *realize a solution*. Possibly you need to do the same thing.

3. Seek Professional Help If Necessary

The third step is something a lot of Christians don't want to talk about; that is to seek professional counseling if necessary.

If you are experiencing a problem with low self-esteem and it is really crippling you, then you should seek professional counseling. Seeking professional counsel is a sign of maturity. You cannot always have the answers within yourself, and the wisdom of a qualified counselor can be invaluable.

You may need professional counseling especially if your low self-esteem is a result of someone else's sin. Recently, I heard the national director of Child Evangelism make a statement that just about shocked the socks off me. He was talking about the effect of sin on children and he said, "In New York City alone, there are twenty thousand boy prostitutes under the age of twelve." *Twenty thousand boy* prostitutes under twelve years of age! They are the victims of someone else's sin.

Possibly you have been the victim of an incestuous relationship. You may have been the victim of physical or verbal abuse as a child. In these instances and in many other instances, a good devotional life may not erase the self-hate that can occur when you are the victim of someone else's sin.

My sister, Jean, is a professional counselor and she offers this advice:

There are certain natural responses to situations we encounter. Emotions and feelings are natural and okay.

A traumatic experience—rape, incest, loss of a loved one through death, divorce—evokes certain responses, feelings, and emotions. I believe that God created us with emotions which we need to accept and deal with.

People can create severe emotional problems for themselves by denying, because they think it is unchristian, their emotions that hurt. Depression for instance, is not unchristian—it is a serious emotional state that needs to be recognized and treated the same as any physical illness. Physical illness is not considered unchristian, so why should we hide emotional problems in the closet and smile like we are on top of the world?

Don't be afraid to seek professional counseling. It is not a weakness and it may be essential. God can use a Christian, professionally trained counselor to begin the healing process.

4. Learn to Accept Praise

Part of accepting yourself is learning the value of accepting praise. This is the fourth step toward more positive self-esteem. I've found that one of the true indicators of a woman's self-esteem is how well she can receive a compliment.

The other day I was out to dinner with my husband and a business associate. In front of this other person, my husband turned to me and said, "My, you look extra lovely tonight." I almost blushed and then said, "Well, thank you. It must be the candlelight in here. It makes everyone look better."

After I said that, I thought, *What am I doing? I'm qualifying myself.* Why couldn't I have just said, "Thank you, Jim. That makes me feel so good. I love you." That would have reminded him to compliment me again sometime. Instead, I reacted with a put-down. In essence, I told him that his eyes couldn't tell the difference between beauty and candlelight.

Low self-esteem always leads with its chin. People with low self-esteem put themselves down and demean themselves. When others try to raise their value they cannot accept it.

I was being interviewed on a television talk show recently and I complimented the man in charge on the handsome suit he was wearing. He said, "Well, it really makes me feel guilty to wear this suit when I think of all the starving people in India." You can be sure that stopped our conversation cold! I felt like saying, "Oh, really? How long has it been since you've sent money to India?"

Correctly accepting a compliment is the mark of a confident woman.

5. Find a Meaningful Cause

The fifth step toward better self-esteem is to get involved in a meaningful cause. It can be any cause you are interested in, but the greatest cause of all is the cause of Jesus Christ.

Get involved in something that will change lives; nothing can bring greater satisfaction. It is so easy to say, "Well, I'll just wait for another time," or, "I'm really busy right now so it must not be God's will for me to teach Sunday school this time." Do you ever do this?

Don't let excuses stop you. If you cannot bring yourself to do something to help someone else, you've got low self-esteem. To remedy this, get involved with something as soon as possible.

According to Viktor Frankl, a Jewish psychologist who was in a concentration camp during World War II, only 5 percent of the people in the camps came out alive. But, that 5 percent possessed a desperate reason to live. They each had a cause. They all had something they wanted to do for humanity.

Your cause may be as simple as becoming involved in your church, forming a car pool in your neighborhood to help working mothers, or doing volunteer work like delivering food to the needy.

Whatever it is, *get involved.* Do something for someone else. I can promise that the rewards will far outweigh the time and energy you put into it.

Remember Acts 20:35 where Jesus says, ". . . It is more blessed to give than to receive" (KJV).

6. Change Your Appearance

The sixth step in bettering your self-esteem is to change the way you look. It is important to understand that your self-esteem is vitally connected with your appearance. It is difficult to like yourself if you're unhappy with the way you look.

Some Christians think it is wrong to be concerned with the body and outer appearance. I disagree. I've seen giant steps in self-acceptance come from those who began to improve their exterior.

One of my Image Improvement students lost forty pounds and her self-esteem soared. Another student, a teenager with a terrible case of acne, went to a dermatologist and got it cleared up. What happened to her self-esteem was phenomenal.

I also had an elderly woman in class who exercised her body into shape for the first time in her life and has never felt better. Another woman had reconstructive breast surgery following the trauma of a mastectomy.

These women are living proof that an outer change can definitely cause an inner change.

During the taping of one of my television shows, I was interviewing a plastic surgeon, Dr. John Graham (his wife, Pat, is an Image teacher in Shreveport, Louisiana). Dr. Graham is a wonderful Christian man, and I asked him whether he thought it was wrong for Christians to have plastic surgery.

His answer was this, "Have you ever looked up the word *vanity* to see what it means in Greek? The word *vanity* means 'emptiness or without purpose.' If you are looking your best to bring honor and glory to Christ then you have a purpose and it is not vanity."

You and I represent the Lord Jesus Christ in all we do. We should present ourselves in the best possible way for His sake as well as our own.

7. Learn to Laugh at Yourself

There is one final step you can take to better your self-esteem: *Don't take yourself too seriously.* In developing your self-image learn to laugh at yourself.

Christians can sometimes be a pretty humorless group of people. We need to laugh at ourselves. If you haven't laughed at yourself today, you can bet someone else has!

I had an experience with this when I was in Atlanta and all my luggage was stolen at the airport. ALL of it; and it still hasn't been found. But you know what? It really doesn't matter because clothes and possessions do not bring real peace and happiness.

When I realized my luggage was stolen I called my husband at home and started to cry. He said, "Don't worry, Joanne, God has never failed you yet." At that time I had thirty minutes to get to a shopping center and purchase a suit to wear as I was to speak at nine o'clock the next morning. I found a new suit in time.

When I called my husband back that night to let him know how I was doing he said, "I've called Deanna and I've told her what has happened. But, I told her not to call you because I know it is late there and I want you to get your sleep."

At about one o'clock in the morning my telephone rang. It was Deanna. She said, "Mom, I'm just going to keep you a minute. I know I'm not supposed to call you, but you know I've never listened to Dad! Mom, I want to tell you some things, but please don't get angry. First, I want you to know that I love you, I'm praying for you, and I'm proud of you. The second thing is this: Have you laughed about it yet?"

I said, "Deanna, it's not funny!"

And then she said, "Come on, Mom, laugh. You'll feel so much better if you do. It's another one of those circumstances you can't do anything about!"

Then we both started to laugh and cry, and the relief that came from that was the greatest therapy of all.

God knows what we need. He gave me a daughter to remind me that life does not always have to be serious. I believe that we all need to work on the ability to laugh at ourselves.

Please understand me when I say we ought not to take ourselves seriously. I do not mean that we should treat our responsibilities lightly. I believe that we are to take Jesus Christ very seriously. We may just need a touch of humor in dealing with our own mistakes.

As sinful as mankind is, God still desires that we be fulfilled in every aspect of our lives. Romans 8:15 says, "We should not be like cringing, fearful slaves, but we should behave like God's very own children, adopted into the bosom of his family. . . ." Are you getting excited about who you are?

Romans 12:2 says, ". . . be a new and different person with a fresh newness in all you do and think. . . ." I just love this verse and love to meditate on it.

God is the ultimate Source of your worth, and you are valuable because He says you are. Otherwise, He would never have sent Jesus Christ to die on the cross for your sins. You can love yourself because Christ first loved you.

Remember, the confident woman values herself. Now, let's move on and see how she values her appearance.

Assignment

Rate-Yourself Questionnaire

Answer the questions below by circling the word that most describes how you feel. There are no right or wrong answers. Be as honest as you can.

1. Do you often feel inferior to most of the people you know?

   Never   Sometimes   Often   Always

2. Do you feel guilty because of your mistakes?

   Never   Sometimes   Often   Always

3. Do you ever feel so discouraged that you wonder if anything is worthwhile?

   Never   Sometimes   Often   Always

4. Do you dislike yourself?

   Never   Sometimes   Often   Always

5. Do you feel afraid or anxious when you enter a room where others have already gathered?

   Never   Sometimes   Often   Always

6. Do you have trouble saying no to a salesperson?

   Never   Sometimes   Often   Always

7. Do you give up when the going gets tough?

   Never   Sometimes   Often   Always

8. Do you consider yourself to be generally unhappy with life?

   Never   Sometimes   Often   Always

9. Do you feel guilty taking time to improve your appearance?

   Never   Sometimes   Often   Always

10. Do you feel tense and anxious in the midst of bad circumstances?

   Never   Sometimes   Often   Always

Work on changing any of the areas where you circled *often* or *always*.

Likable Traits

The more yes answers you can give, the better liked you are. Remember, through self-guidance and perseverance, a no can be changed to a yes!

Can you always be depended upon to do what you say you will do?

Yes   No

Do you cheerfully go out of your way to help others?

Yes   No

Do you avoid exaggeration in your conversation?

Yes   No

Do you avoid being sarcastic?

Yes   No

Do you avoid ridiculing others behind their backs?

Yes   No

Do you accept the ideas and plans of others?

Yes   No

Do you try to avoid arguments?

Yes   No

Are you industrious?

Yes   No

Are you enthusiastic, rather than apathetic?

Yes   No

Do you smile a lot?

Yes   No

Do you wear neat and presentable clothes?

Yes   No

Do you avoid finding fault with others?

Yes   No

PART TWO
The Confident
Woman Values
Her Appearance

Learn About:

- How to put together a basic wardrobe
- Helpful shopping tips
- What your body language is saying
- Which exercises are right for you
- Feminine health problems and solutions
- Massage techniques
- Answers to common skin problems
- How to apply makeup
- How to avoid common hairstyling errors
- How to put it all together dynamically!

4

How to Create the Right Clothing Style

Being a woman is marvelous! I want you to believe this too. I hope you can revel in your femininity and enjoy the great things about being a woman.

Recently I received a letter from my Image Improvement teacher, Kathleen Barnard from Poland, New York. She wrote to tell me about one of her students and enclosed a note the student had written.

Kathleen's student was a young widow with one daughter. She took the eight-week Image of Loveliness course and during this time she met a man. Using what she was learning in class, she attracted him. They are now married.

This woman wrote Kathleen a very revealing letter and I want to share it with you.

> I had denied my femininity and had regressed into a "neutered frump" by the time I entered the adult world. Our society's more negative concepts of womanhood had turned me away from my own identity as a female. In high school and college, I had rebelled against being judged by my body, face, etc., by wearing unbecoming, masculine clothes, being overweight, and in general, just looking sloppy. I had come to the conclusion that it was superficial to spend time and money on my appearance. After all, it's what's on the inside that counts. I knew I was right in this thinking, yet why was I so insecure and unhappy in my unfeminine frumpiness?
>
> Becoming a Christian, Bible studies, and my Image Improvement classes, freed me from the dismal rut I was in. I learned that while it's important to try and be beautiful on the inside, it is just as important to be our very best on the outside. We are the Lord's unique creations and have a responsibility to Him to be our best in every way.
>
> No longer denying my femininity and constantly striving to look and be my best, I feel more comfortable and secure with myself, which enables me to reach out to others and forget myself. As I accept myself, I find it easier to accept others. I am now confident as I am working diligently on my inner and outer self. This is essential to successful living.

There *is* a delicate balance between your inner self and your physical attractiveness. Some of this has to do with your clothing style as this often reflects how you feel about yourself.

What type of clothing are you wearing right now? Are you wearing a uniform? The latest fashion? A timeless classic? An original creation? Or something you should have thrown out of your closet a long time ago?

The type of clothing you choose reflects your personality, your job, and your life-style.

Clothing distinguishes the nurse from the construction worker, the secretary from the gardener. It also tells others whether you are flamboyant, conservative, sensible, confident, sporty, or romantic.

In the 1960s we had a whole movement characterized by appearance. Even today if the words *hippie* or *flower child* are mentioned, a visual image immediately comes to mind. The same thing holds true for other clothing images.

We all know that, in most situations, doctors wear white coats, policemen wear blue uniforms, lawyers wear conservative suits, and movie stars wear evening gowns and diamonds, right?

Some clothing images are so firmly planted that we feel uncomfortable with any deviation. My daughter once went to a doctor who wore jeans, a plaid shirt, and a cowboy hat to the office. To Deanna, his attire seemed out of place and unprofessional. The crowning touch came when he removed the cowboy hat and revealed sweaty hair that clung to his head in a ring the shape of the hat. She soon decided this doctor was not for her. However, had she met this man on a ranch or farm, she probably would not have thought twice about his clothing or his sweaty head!

Clothing power should not be underestimated. What you wear is an important part of who you are. At first glance, no one knows what you're like on the inside—it is the outer packaging that draws others to you.

My friend, Helen, always wore jeans and a sweatshirt. A peek in her closet revealed rows of jeans and sweatshirts! Although she is a business person, she had never realized the importance of her attire. Whether she was working, having lunch with her boss, or relaxing at home, she wore—you guessed it— jeans and a sweatshirt!

After reading my book *Dress With Style* (a complete wardrobe book filled with clothing how to's) she realized her wardrobe was not quite adequate for all the situations in her life. After learning which colors looked best on her (also in *Dress With Style*), she began carefully selecting new items for her wardrobe.

After implementing her wardrobe plan, she found herself besieged with compliments from friends and co-workers, her boss promoted her, and her husband takes her out to dinner more often.

She now knows she looks great in all situations, and because of this, others react more positively to her.

Her wardrobe plan started with careful planning and selection. With this planning, you too can get the most for your dollars and save hours of shopping time and "care" in maintaining your clothing.

This basic wardrobe is put together with a few hardworking pieces. They are:

2 skirts	1 sweater	2 jackets
2 blouses	1 pair of pants	1 dress

For a basic wardrobe that will take you from summer to winter, try using fabrics that are seasonal and transseasonal. Choose durable fabric and classic tailoring in your higher priced garments such as jackets, skirts, and pants. *Quality* is the best buy for you. Investing a few more dollars will help to insure several years of wearability.

Choose easy-to-care-for, quality fabrics for your dresses, sweaters, and blouses. This will cut down on your cleaning bill.

Select colors and fabrics that will work together. Don't be too influenced by the "newest" color or this year's popular shade. Select colors that you like, look well on you, and are appropriate for your working or nonworking situation.

The first step is to choose colors you want to work with. It is best to begin with three coordinating colors and stick with them. Your three colors can be whatever you wish, but as an example, let's work with white, ink navy, and dusty pink. Here are the pieces you'd want to begin with:

1 ink navy, medium-weight, gabardine pair of pants
1 ink navy, cotton or silk shirtwaist dress
1 ink navy sweater with scoop, jewel, or V neckline
1 white blazer jacket in soft wool or linen
1 white skirt in soft wool or linen
1 dusty pink skirt in soft wool or linen
1 dusty pink, cardigan-type jacket
1 dusty pink/ink navy/white striped shirt top
1 dusty pink/ink navy/white striped jacketed shirt/blouse (something to be worn tucked in or out)

Here are examples of all the ways you can wear these nine basic pieces:

To complete this versatile, very basic wardrobe, add these accessories:

A practical leather handbag for work.
A dressier handbag for those important evenings.

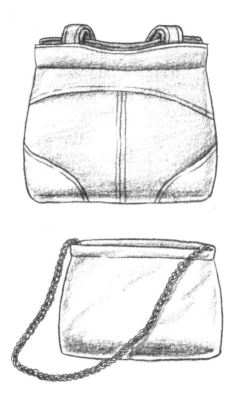

A sporty shoe, a suit shoe, and a dressier sandal, all in leather for longer wearability.

Belts in three widths and in colors that go with your basic pieces.

Scarves in different textures, sizes, and shapes in colors that coordinate.

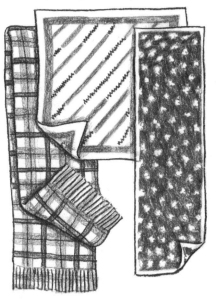

Jewelry basics: pearls, chains. After that, add the fashion neck piece that you have been admiring.

Basics   Fashion piece

If you are a career-oriented woman, you may feel a need for a basic career wardrobe. Your best bet would be a few variations on the basic wardrobe. For you, the basic pieces should be:

2 suits

5 tops

Here are some of the looks you can get with these nine basic pieces:

Dressing for Your Day and Evening World

You may wonder what clothing is appropriate for different situations. Keep in mind that your clothing should reflect your life-style while at the same time help you look your best. Here are outfits for seven days and seven nights, a full week of clothing for the woman who works full- or part-time or at home. Choose your look and event.

MONDAY—Correctly dressed for the morning meeting to begin.

MONDAY EVENING—Playing with the children or grandchildren.

TUESDAY—A brisk walk through the city park on your way to the office.

TUESDAY EVENING— After dinner—relaxing with good friends.

WEDNESDAY—A parent-teacher conference.

WEDNESDAY EVENING—
Last-minute shopping.

THURSDAY—Off to yet another appointment or study group.

THURSDAY EVENING— Quietly relaxing at home.

FRIDAY—Early morning gardening and then off to exercise.

FRIDAY EVENING—A quick snack for you and your loved one before heading for the ball game.

SATURDAY MORNING—
The luxury of a peaceful
moment.

SATURDAY EVENING—
On your way to candle-
light and a romantic dinner
with your man.

SUNDAY—Attending your place of worship.

SUNDAY AFTERNOON—
A calm, thought-filled walk
in the country.

Now that we've covered the basics for your clothing needs and styles, let's take a look at shopping habits. Answering a few simple questions can help you become a wise shopper. Take this quiz and see how you are doing.

1. Do you have an abundance of the same article of clothing in your wardrobe?

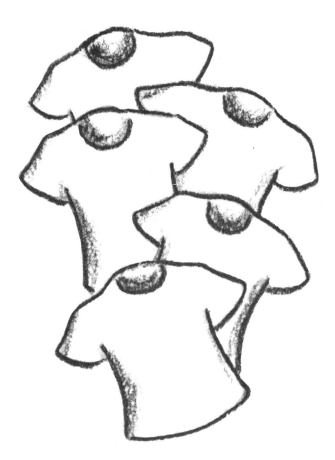

There was a time when my son had *ten* V-neck sweaters in varying colors in his wardrobe. For some reason he couldn't seem to stop buying V-neck sweaters. If you have a tendency to overbuy a certain item, *stop* buying whatever it is you're hooked on. Wait at least one year before you purchase the item again—in moderation.

2. Do you only buy clothing that is inexpensive or "cheap"?

If you do, you probably have a closet full of "great buys" that you never wear. A "great buy" does not necessarily mean you've gotten a bargain. Often the merchandise is inferior and will not hold up past the first few washings. Make sure you are buying a quality item—it will be worth it in the long run.

3. Do you only shop in one department?

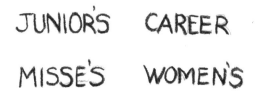

If you always shop in the Junior department (or whatever department), you probably have a limited style. Try shopping in another department for a change. Enjoying a new look doesn't mean you have to abandon the other.

4.   Do you avoid shopping in the accessory department?

Accessories are the key to a versatile wardrobe. They can make or break an outfit. You should be shopping for scarves, jewelry, and/or other accessories at least once a season (or twice a year). With classic pieces of clothing you will probably find that your accessories need to be updated more often than your wardrobe.

5.   Are you label conscious?

One day I brought home a blouse that I thought would be perfect for wearing around the house and playing with my grandchildren. When I got home, however, I found that the blouse was to be dry cleaned only. Not too practical for playing with small children!

Read all labels on a garment before you buy it. Find out the fiber content, washing instructions, and the manufacturer's name. This way you'll know what you're getting and if you enjoy it you can look for other pieces by the same manufacturer. This is especially important if you have a hard time finding clothes that fit properly.

6. Do you only shop for special occasions such as a wedding, an office party, and so on?

If so, you probably have outfits that don't coordinate with each other. You are limiting your wardrobe tremendously. You probably feel you "never have anything to wear." If this is the case, begin working on your basic wardrobe (as per instructions at the beginning of this chapter). You may need to work on buying coordinating separates.

7. Do you always shop with the same friend?

Shopping with the same person (husbands and boyfriends included) can limit you from developing your own style. The other person may also have undue influence in an area they aren't qualified in. Start to trust your own instincts—or at least get more than one opinion.

8. Do you toss out catalogs as "junk"?

You may be missing out on a good way to save money on some of your wardrobe needs. If you shop through the mail make sure you are dealing with a reputable company that sells quality items. Catalogs can be time and money savers if you know how to use them wisely. A word of caution: Catalogs don't give you the chance to try on an item—be prepared that it may not fit and you may need to return it.

Learning about some of your shopping habits can help you avoid mistakes and get the most out of your shopping time. Your own personal clothing style will determine where you shop, but making wise purchases is important anywhere.

In this chapter I've covered many ways in which you can begin to change your appearance. Your wardrobe is just one of the ways you tell others about yourself. Now let's move on to some of the other areas as you learn to fulfill your potential.

5

Body Messages

Let's pretend I've just met you for the first time. I approach you at a snail's pace, with a scowl on my face, and my arms crossed in front of my body. When I reach you, I say, "Oh, I'm so glad to meet you!"

Would you believe me? Probably not. Although my voice said I was glad, my body language said I was reluctant and unhappy.

You believe what you see more than what you hear. What others see in you is what they believe. You are constantly giving off nonverbal clues. As long as this is true, you might as well give off the correct body messages.

Your body language is crucial in dealing with people. It lets them know how you are feeling about yourself and others. This letter from a student of Liz Lundmark, an Image teacher in Lake Oswego, Oregon, will show you what I mean:

Dear Image Improvement,

I want to thank you for changing my life. Before entering your classes I was unconfident and self-conscious of my height—I'm six feet tall. I needed to learn grace and etiquette because I was very awkward due to my sudden growth.

Image Improvement helped me in all of my weak spots and especially in my tall figure. I learned what I should wear for my figure and which colors looked good on me and I gained a lot of self-confidence.

As a freshman at a high school which is bigger than any school I had previously attended, I have participated in the soccer program and I am now actively involved with basketball.

I have met many new people this year, most of them becoming close friends. I thank you, Image Improvement, for making this all possible.

Sincerely,
A walking-tall teen

69

You can tell that this teen has decided to accept her body. She has learned that her body language is critical in telling others about herself, and now she is confident enough to meet new people and win others to her. She is even confident enough to go out in front of others and play competitive sports.

Your body language is critical in letting others know how you feel about yourself. Your body communicates through your face, eyes, hands, posture, and body positions. Let's take a look at these areas individually.

Facial Expression

You've probably heard the old saying, "Your face is your fortune." For some people (models in particular) this may actually be true. However, I'd like to change the old expression and say, "Your face is your forecast." Your face is like the old-fashioned town crier, the one who proclaimed the latest news to all within earshot. Your face forecasts to others how you are feeling and what they can expect from you. Of course, the message received may not be the message you intended to send. To remedy this, take a look at the following facial expressions. Learn about some expressions to avoid and one you may want to cultivate.

Arrogant Look

Deadpan Look

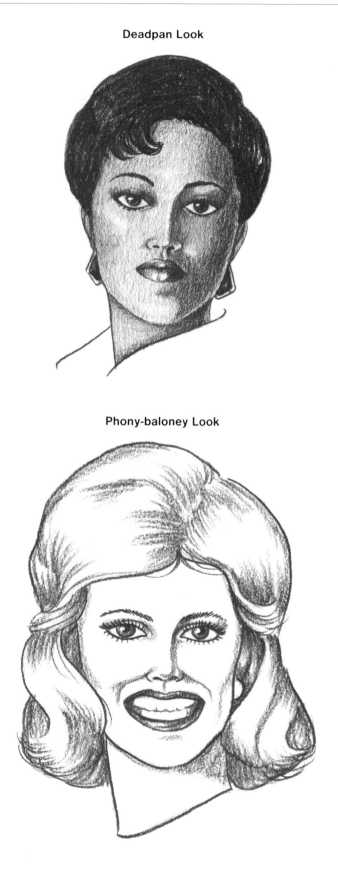

Phony-baloney Look

Worried Look

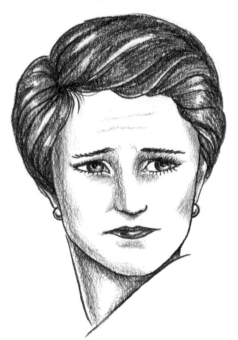

Pleasant Expression

When you are with others, it is important to remember that your face should be animated. Animation is the literal translation of enthusiasm.

This animation is often shown through your smile. When you enter a room your face is on display for all to see. A pleasant look can go a long way toward leaving a good impression.

Use a simple, sincere smile. If your face is aching, you are smiling too hard. However, smiling is important even if you don't always feel like it. Researchers have found that facial expressions can actually *cause* the emotion they portray.

For example, raising your eyebrows, widening your eyes, opening your mouth, and dropping your jaw can actually make you *feel* frightened. In the same way, smiling can help you to *feel* happy.

I'm not saying you should always smile no matter what the circumstances; however, others shouldn't have to suffer through your "blah" days just because you don't "feel" like smiling. You never know when others may be counting on you. I found this out recently when I was returning home after speaking at Coral Ridge Presbyterian Church in Fort Lauderdale, Florida. My flight was late getting into Chicago, and I missed the connecting flight home to Portland.

I went to the airline ticket counter so I could be reboarded on another flight and I began to talk with the ticket agent. As nicely as possible, I told him I'd missed several connections and the airlines had even lost my luggage temporarily just in the past three weeks. I told him I knew it wasn't his fault, it was just a run of bad luck I was having.

The ticket agent listened politely to my complaints and then booked me on the next flight, which had me arriving in Portland too late to give an opening talk at another engagement.

Three hours later, as I was sitting in the boarding area waiting for my flight, this same agent came up to me and said, "Mrs. Wallace, haven't I seen you on Channel 38 here in Chicago? You know, the Christian television station?" Stunned, I said, "Well, yes, but it's been a while!"

He then continued, "Well, I just wanted to thank you for not blowing it. So many of the people who appear on Christian television talk one way and in times of stress, for example here in this airport, they don't live it. Thank you for not blowing your witness."

When he had finished, I said to him, "Whew! Thank you for reminding me!" I really needed that reminder because I *had* almost blown it! I was feeling very ill and tired that day and could very easily have taken it out on that ticket agent. That time I was too close to blowing it! Thankfully, I breathed a silent prayer to say, *Thanks, God, for the reminder that Christians should live what they speak!*

You never know when your slightest conversation will make or break a positive impression. To help in your conversing with others, remember to nod your head in agreement and encouragement. A frozen face and head are an annoyance. Show your interest by smiling and moving your head in response to what others say. But, be careful not to overdo it, as it may appear phony or distracting.

If you are wondering how you are doing with your facial expression, go look in a mirror. What do you see? Are the corners of your mouth turning up or down? Through bad habit and heredity the corners could be turning down. If so, you may be communicating anger, disinterest, or rejection.

For positive communication, work on having the corners of your mouth turn upward (even the slightest bit helps). You don't need to smile outright, but your basic expression should be pleasant.

Eyes

Your eyes are an important part of your facial expression and they need to be dealt with separately. Second only to your voice, your eyes are the most powerful means of communication. Eye contact binds you to the person you are conversing with. Each person you talk to, whether one-on-one or in an audience of thousands, needs and wants to feel important. Eye contact is an essential part of effective communication.

The old saying, "The eyes are the mirror of the soul," gives you some idea of what it means to convince others not only with your words, but with your eyes as well. If you fail to meet the eyes of the person you are conversing with, you will project disinterest, insincerity, distrust, and a lack of confidence. Only by looking directly at another person can you show them that you are sincere in what you are saying.

A woman once came into my Image Improvement office and began trying to "sell" me on why I should carry her line of cosmetics in my company. As we spoke, I inquired as to the length of time her company had been in business and why she felt her company was superior to any others. I wanted to find out if she represented a reputable company.

Although this woman was a professional, she was unable to answer my questions with any direct eye contact. She would look down or all around the room, but never at me. I kept thinking, *What is she hiding?* and I decided against any association with her company.

Another time I had to confront a business associate about a matter involving her honesty and integrity. She exclaimed loudly that she was "not guilty," but she could not look me directly in the eyes as she said it. No matter how many times I tried to bring her gaze to mine she had to look away.

In time it became apparent that she had lied to me and she could no longer be associated with my corporation. Later, I found out that this was a real problem with her and her lack of honesty was evident in her lack of eye contact.

Before you get the wrong idea, let me make it clear: When you converse with someone you should have eye contact with them but don't STARE at them. Staring can make someone feel uncomfortable and self-conscious.

When you converse, your eyes should look into the receiver's eyes, glance up to get a thought, or down to think, and then back to the receiver. This is relaxing to the person who is receiving the message.

For an excellent lesson on good eye contact, watch television actors. You'll notice actors will hold the eyes of the person they are talking to, glance away, then for real emphasis, they will look straight at the other actor. This lets you know they are about to make an important point.

Much research has gone into the area of eye communication. It is now generally accepted that there are basic eye patterns that people use in communication. Take a look at what some of the eye patterns depict:

A dilated pupil (left) as opposed to a normal pupil (right), is considered more attractive and also lets someone know you are interested in them. It is said that just looking at someone you like will dilate your pupil!

Glancing upward to the left means you are recalling a visual memory. If the eyes are rolled upward, it would mean boredom or even sarcasm. (This is for a right-handed person.)

Looking downward signifies a person is talking to themselves. It also shows a lack of interest and possibly boredom. If a person is constantly looking down while they converse, they may also be dishonest or at least uncomfortable with what they are saying.

Looking sideways signifies that a person is listening. It can also be a flirtatious look.

This wide-eyed look signals that a person is shocked, surprised, or bewildered. It can also depict a "sizing up" if it is accompanied with an upward and downward sweep of the eyes as they observe a person or object.

These eyes say, "I like you." They project warmth and acceptance. This is what your eyes should be saying most of the time.

For the most effective eye communication possible, your eyes should mirror your innermost thoughts. This is what I call "heart depth." This is the communication that comes from the sensitive spot in your heart where you feel emotions of love, compassion, and empathy. When someone stirs this feeling in you, you will feel a surge of energy and warmth (possibly even goosebumps) and you'll know that person has touched your heart.

When Aron was two years old he came to stay with me for a whole week (to my delight!). One day we went to a restaurant for a cup of hot cocoa for him and coffee for me. After placing the cups on the table I realized that we didn't have any napkins so I went back to the counter to get them.

When I returned to the table I looked into Aron's face and saw horror in his eyes. He didn't utter a sound, his eyes said it all.

My eyes went to the table and I saw that his entire cup of hot cocoa had been accidentally knocked to the floor. As I looked back to Aron I said, "It's okay, we'll clean it up and get you another. Don't worry, it was an accident."

Immediately his eyes turned from stricken eyes of horror to eyes filled with relief and gratitude. He still hadn't uttered a sound and he didn't cry, but his eyes told the whole story.

Aron used eye communication to touch my heart. Remember, that is the most effective type of nonverbal communication. Work on reaching another person with love, empathy, and compassion. You'll know when the "eyes" have it!

Presence

I prefer the word *presence* to *posture* as people have been using the word *posture* for many years and it often has negative connotations. Instead, let's cover how to have the most effective body presence.

Your body presence is important in talking or listening to another person. Everybody has what experts call "body space," and it is good to keep this in mind when dealing with others. As a general rule, keeping a distance of one and a half to two feet from another person is comfortable for one-to-one conversation. If you are six to eighteen inches from a person you are in the "intimate" zone and this should be reserved for special people in your life. Acquaintances may feel uncomfortable or intimidated if you are too close.

On the other hand, if you keep too much distance between you and the person you are talking with, you will project the idea that you are insincere or not really interested in them.

Watch out for nonverbal clues that will tell you if you are too close or too far away. If you are too close, people may lean back, become rigid, or blink rapidly. You may notice them shift uncomfortably.

If you are too far from people, you may notice them leaning toward you, raising their voices a pitch higher in volume, or even moving closer to you.

Be considerate of others in this area. Some people can accept closer contact with acquaintances than others. Be observant and watch what the other person is doing.

When you are conversing with someone, or even listening, always lean *slightly forward* with your body. This gives the impression that you are interested and sincere. If you lean back, or take a small step away from people, they may perceive you as insincere or not interested in them. Remember that everyone wants to feel important. No one wants to feel rejected. Tell people you talk to that you accept them by leaning toward them.

Nonverbal communication and impatience is another area to be alert to. Watch for jingling keys, jangling coins in the pocket, clicking a pen, tapping a pencil on the table, drumming fingers, or crossed legs with one leg swinging vigorously. These can all be signs of boredom or impatience.

One day as I was waiting in line at my bank I noticed the man in front of me who was very impatient in his body language. He was nice to the bank teller as he talked with her, but his nonverbal clues betrayed his true feelings. He tapped his pencil on the counter, shifted from one foot to another, and at times put his hand into his pocket and jingled his keys.

Be careful about some of the ways you may show your boredom. Be alert to the ways others may show you they are bored. This can save hurt feelings later on.

If you are in a business situation, you need to know that taking notes during a conversation can be very good nonverbal communication. It shows that you are fully involved in what is being said and it is so important to you that you've got to write it down for future reference.

To become an effective note taker, remember these points:

1. Never doodle on your paper with line or circle drawings. This says that you have lost interest in what is being said. You will lose rapport with the speaker, who will feel that you are insincere.
2. Don't take so many notes that you are always a thought behind and have to ask the speaker to repeat every sentence. That is carrying a good thing too far!

3. Don't let the speaker know if you are making a grocery list or writing a letter to Aunt Dorothy! If you write notes, make sure they apply to what is being said, otherwise rudeness is the only nonverbal impression made.

Your body presence also includes the way you walk and stand. The only way to stand is with your hands down to your side. You should use your hands when you are speaking, but if you are listening or not making a point with your hands, leave them at your sides. Don't let them dangle in front or behind you, but directly at your sides. This shows that you are open and sincere. It also exudes confidence and self-assurance.

When walking, think about moving with grace and ease. I would even go so far as to suggest the old schoolgirl exercise of putting books on your head. Stand opposite a mirror and walk toward it, balancing the books as you go. The first few steps will probably alert you to any changes you may need to make. Any jerkiness or sloppy posture will immediately show as the books come tumbling to the floor.

At one time I was working with a contestant for the Miss Oregon scholarship pageant. We drilled with balancing books every single day. Soon she began to walk with a new grace and confidence—even without the books! As she began to walk confidently, she also began to *feel* confident. Her personality became more outgoing and warm. Her shyness began to disappear.

Grace is a state of mind. It is an inner calmness that comes with confidence. And remember—confidence can be learned. Grace is also evident in small gestures. Someone with grace never tugs at her clothes or her jewelry or fusses with her hair. Nor does she check herself in the mirror or replenish her makeup in public. The only exception to this is the discreet application of lipstick without a mirror.

To walk with confidence, place your heel down first, transferring the weight to the arch, then rolling it to the ball of the foot. Move effortlessly, almost like you're on wheels. Walk with your feet pointed straight ahead and fairly close together. You should walk as though you are on a narrow path. It should be an easy, flowing, graceful walk.

One sure giveaway of your age is your walk and movement. Are you flexible and limber? Do you move gracefully?

Watch a young woman walk down the street. You'll notice that everything moves. Her arms swing and her pelvis rotates as her legs stride. In contrast, most older women move their bodies very little. They take shorter steps and bend forward.

What happens when you get older? You develop a tightness in your hip muscles and your upper torso becomes less limber. To counteract this, practice walking with an exaggerated gait—swinging your arms and shoulders forward as the opposite leg strides forward. Take long, purposeful steps.

To improve pelvic mobility, sit on the floor with your legs outstretched in a V position. Bend your knees, touch the soles of your feet together, and grasp the feet with both hands. Bend over slightly so the elbows rest on the inner knees. Gently press down with your elbows, trying to lower your knees to the floor.

Do not bounce or force. Hold this for about fifteen seconds, pressing enough to feel the pull on the inner thighs. Repeat five times.

To strengthen and flex the upper back, an area that is stiff in many women, lie on the floor on your stomach with two or three pillows under your abdomen. With arms at the sides, palms up and resting on the pillows, inhale. Exhale. Raise the head and chest off the floor until the spine is straight. Do not arch. Hold. Count to six. Return to the floor and relax. Repeat five times.

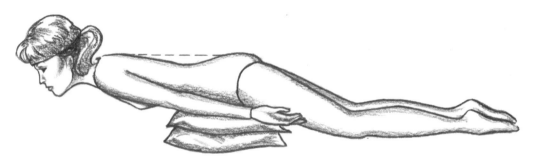

By doing these exercises daily you will develop a new limberness. This will carry over into your walking and body movements. Before long you'll be moving smoothly, gracefully, and confidently. (*Note:* Please don't try these exercises without checking with your doctor first.)

Hands

Your hands should be valued tools in your communication with others. They can show how interested and positive you are.

If possible, keep your hands open and up when using them—this shows that you are not hiding anything.

Generally, the palm up means yes or acceptance. The palm down means no or rejection. Oftentimes, when I say no to someone, or no way, my palm is down and I move my hand straight across in a forceful motion.

Try to say no with your palm up . . . even the tone of your voice will want to say yes.

Bert Decker, founder of Bert Decker Communication Seminars (San Francisco based), has a humorous way of attaching names to many of the incorrect ways of using your hands. Here are some of the gestures he describes and uses in his seminars. Remember, these are all incorrect and should be avoided.

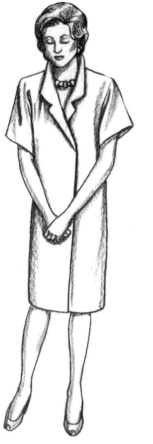

The Fig Leaf gesture

The Stern Mother/Father gesture

The Parade Rest gesture

The Hand Wash gesture

The Prayer of Mercy gesture

Of course, there may be times when you will use these gestures to make a point or to depict an action. However, most of the time you should avoid them.

You may be wondering whether you should talk with your hands at all. The answer is YES. Conversing with your hands shows intelligence and enthusiasm. This is not pantomiming. Pantomiming is usually much too exaggerated for daily conversation.

Your hand gestures should be appropriate to what you are saying and should add emphasis to your words.

Gestures should come in clusters. Be careful not to "read" another person's gestures out of context. Try to understand what the whole thought is about. Look at the whole person.

One final thought about hand gestures: Don't rest your face on your hand(s), either holding your chin or rubbing your eyes, while you are talking with a business associate or acquaintance. This gesture is casual and intimate. To a business associate it can give off an attitude of boredom, sleepiness, and/or insecurity. Be careful with this gesture even when you are with good friends, as you won't want them to misinterpret it.

Body Positions and Signals

Although some people may not believe in body language, the truth is that a person who develops skills in this area will succeed far more often than the person who scoffs at it. You are constantly giving off nonverbal clues about how you are feeling; understanding these clues will help in your relationships with others. Here are some of the most common body positions and their meanings. Memorize them and you will have the inside track in your communication with others.

This gesture indicates some sort of evaluation or meditation. If the body is leaning forward, the person is interested; if the body is leaning back, the evaluation is probably of a suspicious nature.

Covering or concealing the mouth while speaking can mean a person is lying or trying to cover up something. If someone promises you something with her mouth covered, don't count on it.

Steepling the fingertips is an expression of confidence. It indicates that a person is very sure of herself. The more a person "steeples" and the higher the hands are held, the more confident the person feels.

If a person is leaning back and holding her hands and knees, she is feeling insecure and needs to be reassured.

This person is defensive. Her legs and arms are crossed and this signals disagreement, disapproval, and even anger. Learn to recognize this position as it can help you to avoid a more complicated situation later. (Disregard this gesture if you are seated outdoors in freezing weather—it could only signal that the person is cold!)

This look says, "What was that again?" This is often a means of gaining time so the person can gather her thoughts.

This is the typical gesture of honesty. When a person uses this gesture she is trying to tell you that she is sincere. It is the "who me?" pose of innocence. To determine whether the person is really honest or innocent, look at the rest of her body language. Does she look you in the eye when she says something, does she conceal her mouth when she talks?

This woman is bored. It is evident in the way her head is in the palm of her hand and her body position. She can't wait to get out of there!

This body position is evident in a woman who wants to attract a man. It says, "I'm interested in you." Note the way she is looking out of the corners of her eyes—a typically flirtatious look.

This woman is expecting to see someone she is very close to. Note the way she is leaning forward and toward the direction she is looking. She is obviously anxious to have the other person appear.

Along with body positions, there are other nonverbal signals in your communication with others. Here are a few common signals and what they mean:

SIGNAL	WHAT IT MEANS
Smiling when you are speaking seriously.	You are insincere, teasing, or confused.
Tapping your foot, fiddling with your hair, twisting your scarf or jewelry.	You're nervous.
Smiling at nothing for no reason.	You're superficial and insecure.
Scrutinizing, clipping, biting, or doing anything with your fingernails.	You're afraid—and unattractive at the same time.
Cocking head to one side when you speak, or sitting on one leg.	You haven't grown up yet, you're still a child.
Rummaging through your handbag during a meeting or while talking with someone.	You're bored.
Checking yourself in the mirror while talking with someone.	You feel inferior and insecure. You are also rude.

Now that you have learned about some of the most common ideas about body communication, you may find areas you need to work on. There is one ground rule to keep in mind as you practice your new nonverbal communication: BE YOU . . . BE REAL. Nothing is more of a turnoff than to see a phony or plastic person. Be yourself—but be your *best* self. Let your personality and feelings come through your communication with others. Let the body that God created shine in all its uniqueness.

Yes, it is what's on the inside that counts—but it is also what's on the outside that shows!

6

Exercise and Health for Your Well-Being

I just went jogging and now my body feels taut, tingly, and terrific. It feels so good, I can't figure out why I don't go more often. Regular exercise makes me feel great. It's not only healthy for my body, but it helps me look great too!

With all the pluses involved in exercise, why don't more people do it? Granted, the physical fitness craze is sweeping the nation; but there are still a lot of physically inactive people out there.

You've probably heard Romans 12:1 quoted many times before. Even so, it's important, so here it is again: "I urge you therefore, brethren, by the mercies of God, to present your bodies a living and holy sacrifice, acceptable to God, which is your spiritual service of worship" (NAS).

The Lord wants your body. He wants to work through your brain, eyes, ears, lips, arms, and legs. He wants you as a "living sacrifice." In other words, *ALIVE*.

Sometimes we wait until we're sick, incapacitated, or worn out before we offer our bodies (usually to ask for a healing touch). It is better to offer your body then, than not at all; but still, it is best to offer your body when you are strong, vigorous, and in top working order.

When God required sacrifices from His people (in bibical times), He would accept nothing but the best. The leftovers and second-raters were unacceptable. God asked for the "cream of the crop," the first fruits of their labor.

Are you giving God your best? Is your body in the best shape it can be? If not, you may want to consult with your doctor and start an exercise program to help you become all God intended you to be.

Most physical fitness experts agree that aerobic exercise is the best way to firm and tone your body. This type of exercise gives your heart and lungs a workout along with your other body muscles.

Aerobic exercise includes any activity that raises your pulse rate to your own personal "training zone." To determine this zone, subtract your age from 220, then take two-thirds of that number. This is your training pulse rate.

It is important to note that not only do you need to reach your training zone, but you must continue at that pace for at least twenty minutes, four times a week, if you want the full benefits of aerobic exercise.

Aerobic activity is not a stop-and-start affair; it is continuous action. It includes such exercise as cycling, jogging, and brisk walking.

Exercise takes time. But, it doesn't need to take as much time as you might have thought. If you feel you are too busy for a regular exercise program you may want to consider these suggestions:

1. Schedule your exercise just as you would any other appointment. If you plan ahead you should be able to budget time for it.
2. Try getting up half an hour earlier in the morning just to exercise. (Read on for ways to get you going in the morning.)
3. Always keep leotards and tights (or other suitable exercise attire) in your desk drawer or tote bag. That way if you find yourself with available time, you'll be ready.
4. If you can't manage time for a whole workout, try closing your office or bedroom door and "take ten." Especially good for the upper torso are push-ups done leaning against the wall.

You may also want to try these "lazy day" exercises. They help you wake up and get you ready to go. (Please check with your doctor before attempting these exercises.)

1. Lie flat on the bed with your arms over your head. Stretch one side of your body from head to toe and then switch to the other side. Repeat this two or three times until you are shifting easily from side to side.

2. Place your hands behind your head. Slowly pull forward until you feel the back of your neck begin to stretch. Lower your head gently back.

3. Lay your arms flat at your sides. Raise one leg and point your toes to the ceiling. Stretch high. Lower your leg slowly. Repeat with other leg.

4. Lying flat, bend your knee and bring it slowly toward your chest. Keep your other leg straight. Repeat with the other leg.

5. Start by lying flat with your knees bent and your feet apart. Raise pelvis and then support buttocks with your hands. Gently lower your body and repeat three times.

Starting a new exercise program has its disadvantages—sore muscles and uncomfortable aches and pains. You may even risk injury.

To reduce the chance of muscle soreness or injury, start exercising gradually and always begin with five minutes of stretching exercises. Here are some basic stretching exercises that can also be used for exercising certain areas of the body.

Fit and Trim Posture

Step 1.   With your feet apart, bend over from the waist and let your arms hang down loosely.

Step 2.   Arch your back and raise your head, extending right arm forward and up, left arm back and up.

Step 3.   Assume bend-over position, then repeat the extension with left arm forward.

Note: As your posture improves, so will your bustline. Most exercises that are designed to tone those muscles that support the breasts will also help your posture. Many of the exercises on these pages do double duty.

Hip Exercise

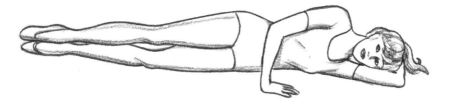

Step 1. Stretch out on floor on left side with head pillowed on left arm. Put right hand on floor for support.

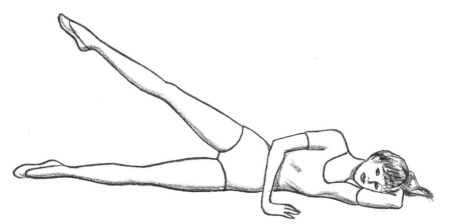

Step 2. Raise right leg as high as possible with knee straight, toes pointed. Repeat several times, then switch sides.

Tummy Exercise

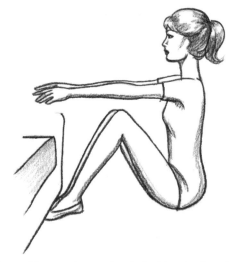

Step 1. Sit on the floor with your knees bent, feet hooked under a sofa or a low rung of a chair, arms extended in front of you.

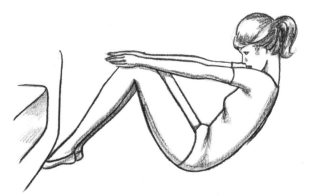

Step 2. Drop your chin toward your chest, round your back, and roll down on the floor slowly, trying to touch the floor with only one vertebra at a time. When your back is flat on the floor, extend your arms overhead and relax for a few seconds.

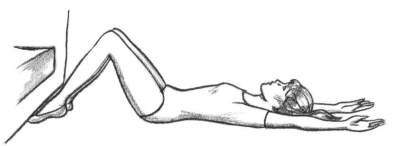

Step 3. Throw your arms forward and rise slowly, with your chin tucked in. Straighten back and raise your head. You should now be back to the original position.

Waist Exercise

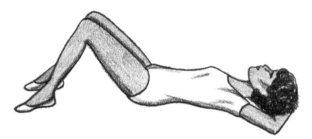

Step 1.   Lie on the floor with knees bent, feet flat on the floor about six inches apart, and hands clasped behind head.

Step 2.   Sit up and twist around until you can touch left elbow to right knee.

Step 3.   Resume first position, then sit up and touch left knee with right elbow.

Thigh Exercise

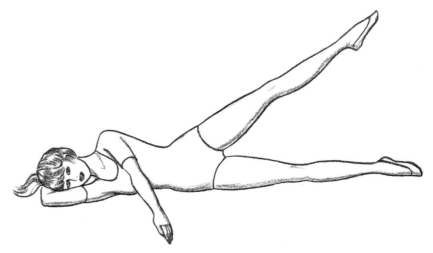

Step 1.   Lie on side and with head resting on bottom arm, keep other arm straight out in front of you. Keeping legs straight and toes pointed, raise and lower upper leg four times.

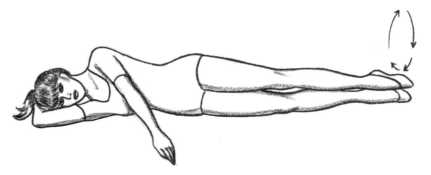

Step 2.   Now make four circles with upper leg, moving it forward, up, back, and down again to the starting position.

Step 3.   Next, lift top leg straight up a few inches, bring bottom leg up to meet it, lift both legs together another few inches, and return legs together, slowly, to floor. Alternate side.

To start with, exercise regularly but not every day. A good program for a beginner is a thirty-minute workout four times a week. To this, add 10 percent per session—for a thirty-minute workout, add three minutes per session until you are at the level you desire.

To ease any muscle soreness that may occur, try a long hot soak in a tub or Jacuzzi; a physical massage or external muscle balm such as Ben-Gay. Stiff or sore muscles occur within eight to forty-eight hours after exercise and should not be confused with sudden pain or soreness that could signal an injury.

If you are injured, don't try to exercise through the pain. Instead, use this simple treatment called RICE (**R**est, **I**ce, **C**ompression, and **E**levation). It is good for bruises, sprains, and pulled muscles. If your injury seems more serious or pain persists see a doctor.

For minor injuries, here's what to do:

1. Rest—Stop exercising and don't use the injured part unless absolutely necessary. Use crutches, a sling, or splint if the injury requires it.

2. Ice—Pack the injury with ice for twenty to thirty minutes. Do this every two hours for forty-eight hours after the injury.

3. Compression—Wrap the injury with an elastic bandage. You'll know the bandage is too tight if you notice a pins-and-needles feeling.

4. Elevation—Elevate the injury above your heart if at all possible.

Remember, most minor injuries can be prevented by starting out slowly and gradually building on your exercise routine. Taking it slowly helps to insure that RICE will never be necessary!

Exercise should be fun. It should be an exciting part of your routine. In order to add this excitement, you may need to counterbalance your work situation with your activities. The chart on page 102 may be helpful in choosing the right activities for you. Take a look, you may discover some new ideas for making the most of your recreational time.

Even in the area of exercise and recreation we are all unique. Basically, I am not an exercise person. It is hard for me to stay on an exercise program. My husband is just the opposite. Jim can't understand why anyone wouldn't love to exercise.

For me, Galatians 6:9 has always been important when I think of exercise. You may want to memorize it as part of your own exercise program. It says, "And let us not get tired of doing what is right, for after a while we will reap a harvest of blessing if we don't get discouraged and give up."

Taking care of your body through exercise is an important part of becoming a confident woman. It is also important for staying healthy. However, it is not the only measure of health. It is essential to be aware of the other special health needs that women have.

IF:	TRY:
Your job is repetitious and routine.	Tennis, golf, racquetball, or some sport that requires you to use your mind in order to play well.
You work with machines.	Cross-country skiing or swimming. Anything in or near water will be beneficial as water is definitely not mechanical!
You work on a team.	Bicycling, jogging, or one-on-one games like throwing a Frisbee or chess.
You work alone most of the time.	Team sports, join a softball league or bowling team.
You have to make a lot of decisions.	Planning a nonstructured amount of time for recreation. Enjoy a long walk in the country or roller-skate outdoors.
You are not your own boss.	Supervising a Little League team, jogging or bicycling, taking long uninterrupted walks.
You feel bored and unchallenged.	Exciting forms of recreation such as mountain climbing, scuba diving, or skiing.
You are under stress and tension.	Venting your tension by swimming vigorously, lifting weights, throwing darts, exercising aerobically, or even flying a kite.

One of the most common health problems is menstrual cramps. If you suffer from this problem there is relief available. Try these easy-to-do exercises to help relieve pain and get you back on your feet. (Of course, again, do check all exercises with your doctor before trying them.)

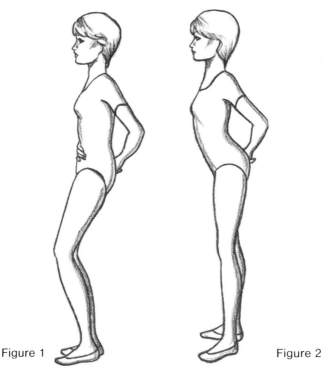

Figure 1   Figure 2

1. **Pelvic Rock**—This helps to ease the dull ache in your lower back and thighs. Stand with your feet slightly apart. Place your palm on your lower abdomen and with the back of the other hand press gently on the small of your back (see figure 1). Relax your shoulders and buttocks. Slowly swing your pelvis forward and bend your knees. You will feel your abdominal muscles tighten. Swing your pelvis back and straighten your knees (see figure 2). Repeat for as long as you need.

2. **Vertical Rest**—This exercise helps to relieve tension which in itself can contribute to cramping. Lie on your back with your knees bent and supported by a pillow. Use a pillow to support shoulders and head (see drawing). Breathe deeply and relax in this position for twenty to thirty minutes. You may even want to try a hot-water bottle on your abdomen while you relax. Heat is an effective cramp reliever.

Another problem that is related to the menstrual cycle is "premenstrual syndrome" or PMS. It is a common condition that occurs in women fourteen to fifty and is characterized by physical and mental symptoms occurring seven to fourteen days before menstruation.

The physical and mental symptoms can include: cramping, breast tenderness, water retention (with resulting weight gain and swollen legs or ankles), backaches, headaches, acne, anxiety, and irritability.

I am told that PMS affects 20 to 30 percent of all women of childbearing age with symptoms severe enough to require treatment. Five percent are so seriously affected they are incapable of functioning for a week or so before their periods.

In the past, treatment for PMS has been limited to counseling, hypnosis, diuretics, tranquilizers, antidepressants, and the ever popular "thinking good thoughts." None of the treatments has worked well and most have failed miserably.

Fortunately, there is a new treatment available which uses a supplemental source of gamma linolenic acid (GLA), the lack of which may be one cause of PMS.

This supplement comes from the oil of the evening primrose flower and some doctors are discovering great success with this treatment. The supplement is provided in the form of capsules and is used with other important vitamins and minerals. The success rate for the treatment of PMS with this supplement is between 60 and 80 percent. The evening primrose oil supplement treatment is showing effects after just two or three months. It is allowing some PMS sufferers to lead normal lives. If you have this problem, check with your doctor about evening primrose oil.

You can find evening primrose oil (which contains GLA) in your local health food store. It is providing answers to women in an inexpensive and easily available method. However, you should never take this kind of supplement without first checking with a doctor.

As a woman, you may also be concerned about the risk of breast cancer. This is a frequent occurrence, but also one that is relatively less dangerous than other forms of cancer if it is detected early enough.

There is a five-minute check you should be doing about once a month to help you detect breast cancer in its earliest and curable stage. It is simple, easy, and does not require a visit to your doctor.

Breast Self-Examination

To examine your right breast, lie down with a pillow under your right shoulder (see drawing). Place right hand under your head. With your left hand, keeping fingers flat, press gently in small circular motions. Check for any changes in the breasts, lumps, hard knots, or thickening. My gynecologist says a hard lump that will not move when touched is cause for concern. Repeat this procedure for the left breast.

To continue the examination, stand in front of a mirror. Look for any dimpling of the breast skin, puckering, or retraction of the nipple. Beginning at the outside top of the breast, move fingers an inch at a time and slowly circle the entire breast, including the nipple. This should require at least three complete circles (see drawing). It is normal to have a ridge of firm tissue in the lower curve of the breast. Repeat for the other breast.

Last, squeeze the nipple and note any discharge either clear or bloody. If you discover discharge, report it to your doctor (unless you are pregnant or breast-feeding). Repeat this on the other nipple.

To avoid other feminine problems such as vaginal infections, make sure you:

1. Only wear underpants that have a 100 percent cotton crotch. Cotton is a natural fabric that allows your body to "breathe," thus reducing the chance of infection.
2. Don't use deodorant soaps on your genital area. Deodorant soaps can leave a strong residue that may irritate your skin and contribute to vaginal infection. Use only 100 percent pure Ivory soap which has no added colors or scents.
3. Use only plain, white toilet paper. The dyes and perfumes in colored or scented paper can also be harmful to the genital area and can increase the risk of infection.

Finally, let's cover a health problem that is often overlooked. I'm talking about stress. Stress is really one of the biggest problems that women face. Since it can't always be avoided it is good to know that there is at least one way to deal with it. My favorite luxury and an important way to beat stress is massage. There is actually nothing quite like it.

Here is how you can become an expert. (P.S. You may want to enlist the aid of your exercise partner, best friend, or husband. If you trade services you'll both benefit!)

Massage

Use this massage for cramped or tight arm muscles. With both hands, hold onto the extended arm and knead the muscles. Move up and down the arm. (When by yourself, work the muscle with your arm held straight by your side.)

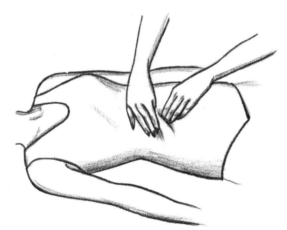

You cannot relax a cramped muscle by pounding on it. Instead, squeeze and roll the skin with your fingers. Use this method on all parts of the body, especially the back and abdomen.

Your joints may need special attention after a vigorous workout. Enlist a friend, or do self-massage on your knees, elbows, and wrist joints. Knead with your fingertips. Keep joints flexed.

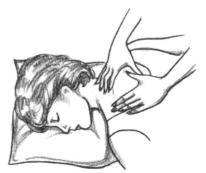

Use the muscle-rolling technique to ease tense muscles in your back. Use firm pressure and roll steadily across any problem areas.

I cannot emphasize strongly enough how important your health and well-being are to your whole outlook on life. It was brought home to me when I was involved in a near fatal car accident and spent months lying flat on my back. Simple things I had taken for granted suddenly seemed monumental. I could not run to my children if they needed me; I couldn't take a leisurely stroll in the country; I couldn't even make it to the bathroom unaided.

I learned then never to take my health for granted. Our bodies are precious gifts, and we should not treat them with indifference.

Remember, God created us as mental, spiritual, and physical beings. All three must be in balance. To become a confident woman, you've got to have confidence in your body. Not only should it be exercised, it should also be safeguarded against disease and stress.

Every time I see the word, *body,* I think of this acronym:

B alanced
O uter
D ynamic
Y ou!

Try thinking of your body in this way and you will be surprised at some of the changes that can occur. You may find your body isn't so bad after all.

7

Face Facts

Healthy skin doesn't just happen. It is not necessarily something you are born with. Healthy skin is the result of proper care.

The basics for healthy skin care have been covered in my first book, *The Image of Loveliness,* and in my second book, *Dress With Style,* but to recap the information, let's look at the products you should be using on your face.

At least twice a day—in the morning and at bedtime—you should be using a cleanser. It should be a water-based cleanser that removes all makeup, oils, and impurities.

You should also be using a moisturizer on your skin (at least twice a day) to replenish lost moisture, plump cells (for fewer wrinkles), and help keep dirt out of your pores.

All the skin-care products you use should be water-based. This means that you apply them with water. Since your body is composed mostly of water, oil-based products can clog your pores. Using water-based products applies to all the skin types—dry, oily, normal, or combination oily/dry.

If you want further information on the basics of skin care, refer to my earlier books or contact the Image Improvement Instructor in your area. You can write to me for her address.

Also, a new line of skin-care products has been released under my name— The Joanne Wallace Collection. To send for a free catalog of products available see page 191.

Once your face is cleansed and moisturized, you are ready to begin the actual application of makeup.

Foundation

Usually by the time a woman reaches the age of eighteen she should be using a makeup base or foundation to even her skin tone. This product should be water-based and give a smooth finish without shine.

Do not try to match foundation to your inner wrist, it is not the same tone as facial skin. To choose the right color, apply the product to a small area of your jawline; this allows you to see how the color will blend with your face and your neck. Try several shades next to each other on your face to see which one is best. Foundation should match the deepest tone in your skin—or go about one shade deeper than your overall skin tone.

To apply foundation, start with just a little bit and then add more if you need it. A heavy coat of foundation looks harsh and unattractive. Keep it smooth and *always blend* the product into your hairline, jawline, and neck. Don't leave a definite mark where the foundation ends.

Use a damp sea sponge to smooth the lines and when you're finished, dust your face with translucent powder. The translucent powder will help set the foundation and will dull any excess shine. Brush off any extra powder.

Eyes

Keep your eye shadow colors in the same color family. Use *powder* shadows. Your eyes are the moistest part of your face, and cream shadows tend to glob and crease.

Don't dust frosted shadows all over your eyelid as a frosted shadow reveals tiny imperfections and wrinkles. It can look unnatural—especially in daylight. Save frosted shadows for underbrow highlighting only.

Always blend your shadows; use your fingers or a dry sponge. The unblended look is artificial and obvious.

Use brown, gray, or black mascara. Try to make sure the lashes are separated. Eyelashes that clump together look messy. To solve this problem, use several thin coats of mascara.

Don't forget about your eyebrows. Pluck any stray hairs and use a pencil to fill in the gaps—or use an old mascara (one that's almost gone) to brush on eyebrows and fill them in.

Don't draw heavy lines under or over the eye. Use an eye pencil and make sure it is a smudged look—not a definite line.

Here are a few examples of how to apply eye shadow to make the most of your type of eye.

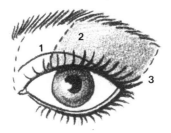

Close-set Eyes

1. Apply light shadow from lashes to brow bone.
2. On outer and upper two-thirds of eye area, apply medium shadow.
3. Line bottom lashes and two-thirds of top lashes with dark pencil.
4. Apply mascara, concentrating on the outer two-thirds of your lashes.

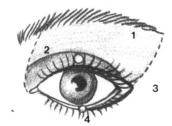

Small Eyes

1. Use a light/neutral shadow from lashes to brow.
2. Use a medium shadow on lid.
3. Outline two-thirds of the eye, extend color above, below, and beyond eye. *Blend well.*
4. Dot your top and lower inside eyelid with an iridescent pencil that matches the color of your eyes. Apply mascara.

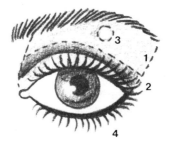

Deep-set Eyes

1. Use light shadow all over lid and brow bone.
2. Apply darker tone of same color just above natural crease. *Blend well.*
3. Dot iridescent highlight just below arch of eyebrow.
4. Use a dark pencil to line lower lid. Apply several coats of mascara.

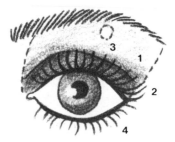

Protruding Eyes

1. Apply light shadow from lashes to brow.
2. Use dark shadow from lashes to crease.
3. Touch highlighter to highest point of brow arch.
4. With dark pencil, line lower lashes. Apply mascara, especially to the lashes just above the iris.

Cheeks

Use a powder blush or a cream rouge, the choice is yours. A cream rouge is usually best for dry skin, and a powder blush is better for normal to oily skin.

To brighten your face, use a slightly darker shade of blush. For darker skin tones, use a more intense color such as deep berry, burgundy, or deep russet.

Your cheek colors should be in the same color family as your natural skin undertones. If your undertones are pink, use colors in the pink family—rose, wine, burgundy, and so on. If your undertones are peach (golden), use colors like peach, coral, russet. Match your cheek color to the intensity of your natural coloring—not too pale or too dark.

Make sure to blend your cheek color. It should look natural, not harsh. Remember, makeup is to enhance, not cover up, your natural beauty.

Here's how to apply cheek color for different face shapes:

Long or Narrow Face

Keep blush concentrated on the sides of the face, then blend slightly onto the temple area.

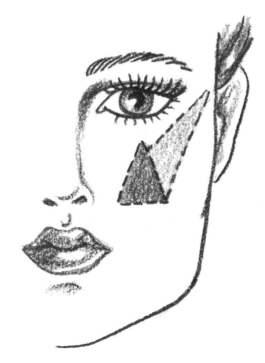

Square Face

Apply just below the cheekbone and blend up sharply. Concentrate color under the eyes.

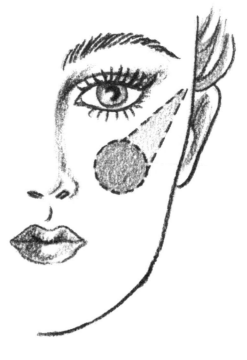

Oval Face

Concentrate color on the apples of your cheeks, blend out following cheekbone.

Round Face

Concentrate color on top of cheekbone, blending up and out. Apply blush first to the darkest area, blending into lighter zone.

Lips

Your lip color should stay within the same color family as your cheek color. If you use pink blusher, choose a lipstick in a pink or wine shade. If your blush is peach, choose a coral or brown shade.

For lip color that lasts, begin by lining the lips with a lip pencil in a shade slightly deeper than your lipstick. Lip liners and lip colors should always coordinate. For longer wear, lipstick should be applied and blotted twice before the final application.

Lips come in all shapes and sizes. To make the most of your lips, follow these guidelines:

Wide Mouth

Avoid extending color all the way to the corners. Apply just inside lip lines.

Thin Lower or Upper Lip

Extend color just beyond lip lines on the smaller lip, just inside lines on the larger lip. Use a slightly brighter color of lipstick (in the same color family) on the smaller lip. Apply lip gloss only to the smaller lip to make it appear fuller.

Tiny Lines Around Mouth

Don't outline your lips in a dark, strong color. Use a soft, translucent color. Blend foundation into lip line to help prevent the color from "bleeding." Avoid frosted or glossy lip colors.

Uneven Mouth

Work toward matching tips of Cupid's bow with nostrils. Color both sides alike even if your color extends past the lip line a little.

Straight Upper Lip

To soften this shape, create a slight bow by extending the color just beyond the upper lip line.

Skin

You may have skin problems that need more than just proper skin care and the right makeup. Here's how to deal with some bothersome problems.

Broken Capillaries and Brown Spots

To minimize broken capillaries, use vasoconstrictive facial masks—those containing rose hips, aloe vera, chamomile, azulene, wheat germ oil, collagen, allantoin, and panthenol.

To minimize brown spots (often associated with pregnancy) and to disguise broken capillaries, use a concealing product. Lydia O'Leary's Covermark provides good coverage. Always apply your foundation over the concealer.

Undereye Circles

Dark circles are inherited. The best way to solve this problem is to conceal them with makeup. Use a foundation cover-up a shade lighter than your usual base. This will lighten the area subtly.

Wrinkles

Wrinkles are caused by the sun. If you want to prevent wrinkles, stay out of the sun! Since this isn't always possible, you can help prevent wrinkles by using a sun block.

If you've already got wrinkles, you can help minimize them. Use a coverstick a shade lighter than your skin tone and dot it around the nose, mouth, and forehead; blend well.

Using softer colors on your cheeks and lips will help make wrinkles less obvious.

For eye wrinkles, use eye shadows in gray or blue tones. Never use heavy makeup or cream shadows. Always treat your eyes gently. Carefully remove makeup and contact lenses.

Enlarged Pores

The size of your pores is a matter of heredity. If you have oily skin or a tendency toward acne, chances are you have large pores.

You cannot shrink your pores, but you can make them seem smaller by using an astringent. This will only work temporarily and must be done on a regular basis.

The best treatment for large pores is cleansing your skin often and thoroughly. Use only water-based products.

Blackheads, Whiteheads, and Pimples

To deal with skin blemishes, you must first understand what they are. Blackheads are oil plugs that push to the surface. When the surface is tightly closed they become whiteheads. A pimple is an inflamed whitehead.

Skin blemishes of all kinds are common for women because of the menstrual cycle and changing hormone levels. Your makeup can also irritate your skin, so make sure you use a product you are not allergic to.

To prevent blemishes, cleansing is essential. Once again, water-based makeup can be the key. Another treatment is using a facial mask. This can help unclog your pores and remove blackheads that can become pimples.

There are many products available that are good for your skin. To help you select the right product, I've listed a few ideas that can turn you into a confident shopper.

1. Remember *you* are in control. Don't let someone pressure you into buying products you don't need or want. Don't spend more than you can afford.
2. When shopping in a department store, look for an organized, well-stocked counter. They should also have samples available for you to try.
3. Choose a sales consultant who is wearing makeup in a way you admire. If you like the way she looks you'll probably agree on basic skin-care ideas.
4. Ask questions. If you don't like the answers or feel uncomfortable with the consultant, wait. Come back another time and meet with a new consultant, or look for a different product line.

Skin care doesn't have to be complicated. It should be a daily part of your routine. Even if you don't wear makeup, good skin care is essential.

Taking care of your skin can put a whole new complexion on life!

8

Hair Treatment

Since prehistoric times, both men and women have spent time and effort arranging their hair. Hairdressing as we know it (cutting, curling, brushing, and adorning) dates as far back as 3,000 B.C.

With all the years since then, it seems amazing that the subject of hair care has not been exhausted. It proves how important and vital hair care is to men and women alike.

Proper hairstyling can often make or break your appearance. Imagine a beautiful woman with elegant clothes, immaculate makeup, and greasy, stringy hair. It sort of ruins the picture, doesn't it?

Take a good hard look at yourself. What do you see? Are you making errors with your hairdo? If so, you should know what to do to correct them.

Very few women are natural beauties. We all have imperfections; but why accent them? There are definite right and wrong ways to style your hair to suit your particular structure, age, and hair quality. Here are a few errors you may be making—and ways to avoid them:

The Error: The Wrong Length for Your Hair Texture

You have very fine hair and wear it long because you think length will give your hair an illusion of fullness. You adore the long, straight, mod look; but your hair just hangs there, looking stringy.

How to avoid this error:

Very fine hair should never be worn longer than collar length and should be styled simply. The mod look may be tempting to you, but hair worn that way needs plenty of body. A short, casual coif will hold its set, giving the hair the look of body.

The Error: Unnecessary Thinning

You have thick, coarse hair and think that thinning will give a smoother, softer look. So, you take yourself to the hairdresser and end up still looking bulky—and with split ends.

How to avoid this error:

Thinning your hair won't solve any problems. In fact, it creates more difficulties. Try either straightening (which works beautifully on coarse hair) and/or letting your hair grow longer. The weight of long hair usually results in a slimmer, sleeker silhouette. Also, so you don't end up with spring-tight curls, set your hair with large rollers for medium to long hair.

The Error: Accentuating a Square Face

You have a square-shaped face and wear your hair pulled back tightly and tied with a scarf or ribbon. It's neat and nice, but you look "all jaw."

How to avoid this error:

The way to slim a prominent jawline is to wear your hair down and curved gracefully over the squarest part of your jawline. This will give your face an oval look . . . and a lovelier one!

The Error: Not Camouflaging a Narrow Forehead

Your forehead is quite narrow. You are wearing your hair pulled back on the crown and secured with a barrette, giving your face a long, skinny look.

How to avoid this error:

Shorten your face and widen your forehead by having bangs cut. Give the bangs *and* the sides of your hair more fullness.

The Error: Making a Moonface Look Even Rounder

You have a very round face, and you're wearing a hairdo that is ear-length—parted in the middle, with flipped-up ends.

How to avoid this error:

A round-faced beauty should avoid a hairdo that emphasizes the fullness of the cheeks. If your hair is long it should fall over the cheekbones in a gentle curve, thus cutting off the chunky cheekline. If you have short hair, keep curls off the face . . . and no higher than the chinline. You can wear curls, but only below the chin or on the shoulders. With a round face you *can* wear a center part, but again, only if your hair is long.

The Error: Too Much Teasing

You're lovely . . . you have a profile that would make Helen of Troy jealous! But you walk around with hair so thoroughly teased that a fellow six inches taller than you can't see over your head!

How to avoid this error:

The answer is *don't tease!* Concentrate on playing up the magnificent line of your face. Sometimes the tendency is to overdo and overmakeup a beautiful woman. But beauty is truly enhanced when it appears as natural as possible. A sleek, simple hairdo that gives the face a clean line and a natural look wins our vote!

The Error: Ears Showing That Should Be Covered

You have a small face and ears that protrude slightly more than normal. Since you like your hair away from your face, you wear it pushed behind your ears, either loose or in a bow and hugging your neck. Very chic . . . except you resemble a little mouse!

How to avoid this error:

Modern innocence can be wistful and feminine. You can have this look, but varied slightly. If your ears are a wee bit bigger than they should be for the size of your face, pull hair partially over ears.

The Error: The Too-old Look for the Too-young Girl

You're a working girl in your mid-twenties who needs to look both neat and mature, so you're wearing your shoulder-length hair in a small bun at the nape of the neck. That middle part completes the picture for the staid, old-fashioned image.

How to avoid this error:

If you're in your mid-twenties and have resigned yourself to the middle part, nape-of-the-neck, bun-look, you need a whole new outlook on life!

Choose a creative hairdresser and get a complete overhaul. New cut, new styling, and new ideas will help you discover how a young woman can look neat and swinging in this modern, on-the-go world! Find the new you!

The Error: Wearing Hair in One Style for Too Long

You have long, straight hair, and find that a French twist is the most attractive for you. During the last five months you've noticed a receding at the hairline behind your ears.

How to avoid this error:

First, never wear your hair pulled back so tightly that you feel the slightest bit of tension. This is one cause of receding hair. Second, hair needs occasional changes in direction and changes in location of the part. There are many fashionable and comfortable hairdos for long, straight hair. If you can't find one other than the French twist, cut your hair!

The right shampoo is important for your hair. Here are a few guidelines to help you know if your shampoo is a good one:

1. You should only need to shampoo your hair once unless it's very oily. Shampoo labels that tell you to lather and rinse twice usually just want you to use the product faster so you'll need to buy more. Lathering and rinsing more than once can strip hair of essential oils.

2. After shampooing, your hair should be soft, shiny, and manageable. If it isn't, your shampoo probably contains too much detergent. You may want to shop for a gentler shampoo.

3. Shampoo should rinse easily and not leave any residue. Residue leaves hair dull and lifeless.

4. Shampoo should not irritate your scalp.

5. Shampoo should be simple to use and satisfy your preference for color, perfume, and lather. Keep in mind that a shampoo does not have to lather in order to clean your hair.

6. You should be able to shampoo your hair every day. Frequent shampooing should not harm your hair if you've chosen a gentle shampoo.

Along with the correct shampoo, styling is also important. Here are three different ways to use your hair dryer like a professional.

Hair Dryer Tips

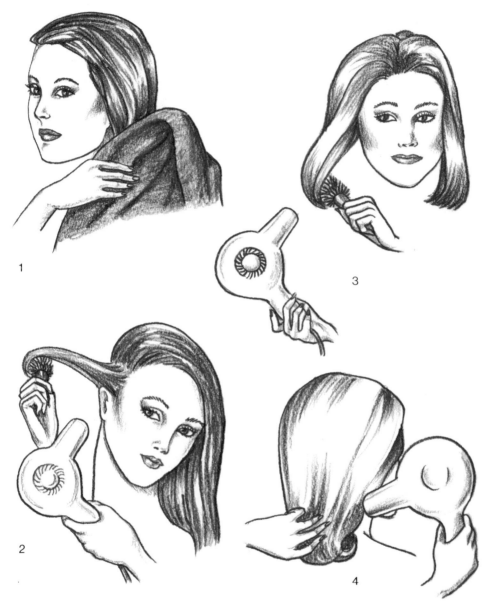

Long Straight Hair

1. Don't tousle your hair as this can cause tangles. Instead, towel dry by squeezing gently until your hair is just damp.
2. Blow a three-inch section of hair at a time. Keep dryer on low heat and aim at roots. With brush, keep hair away from scalp.
3. When roots are almost dry, blow the rest of the hair.
4. Gather hair at the nape of the neck, curl hair under, and blow along the roll.

Short, Layered Hair

1. Towel dry same as described before, then apply setting lotion and blend through hair.
2. To add height and soft curls, use a round brush. Start with the center section of hair at the crown. Pull brush forward, folding hair around brush. Move dryer quickly back and forth across hair.
3. Continue this in sections just big enough to wrap around brush easily. Dry entire head this way.

Straightening Long, Curly Hair

1. Divide hair into eight sections—four in front and four in back. Make more sections if your hair is thick.
2. Wrap each section in a loose pincurl. Fasten and secure temporarily. Beginning at the front, wrap each section around a round brush. Wrap under in back and away from face. Keep hair tight around brush as you blow dry.

Once you've decided on the hairstyle you would like to have, what's next? How can you make sure your hairstylist understands exactly what you want?

Going to a hair salon can be a frightening experience, especially if you are going for the first time, are planning on making a hair change, or you've had a disastrous experience at a hair salon before.

There is a certain vulnerability that accompanies a trip to a hair salon. Outside of your family, who else sees you in quite the same condition as your hairdresser? Let's face it, wearing a plastic cape with a wet head of hair can be embarrassing.

Hair salon fears are widespread. Let's deal with some of the most common fears women face in a hair salon. Maybe one of them applies to you.

First, there is the fear of wanting a new hairstyle but being afraid of looking too different. The key to mastering this fear is to talk it over thoroughly with your hairstylist. Discuss the options and whether the new style will work for you and your type of hair. Weigh your feelings, if you feel more inclined toward the change then go ahead with it; if you feel too unsure, wait awhile. You can always try it next month or next year.

Second, there is the fear of not being able to duplicate the style once you leave the salon. To allay this fear, tell your stylist how much time you have to spend on your hair and which styling techniques you are comfortable doing. Watch closely to see how the stylist does your hair. What type of brush is used, at what angle the dryer is held, where the curlers are placed, and so on. Find out about any technique you're unfamiliar with.

The third fear is going in for a trim and coming out with a cut that is too short. To solve this, make sure you and your hairstylist agree about what is long, medium, or short. Generally, *long* means shoulder length or longer, *medium* means chin to shoulder length, and *short* means any cut that shows the nape of your neck or reveals your ears. If your hairstylist still cannot give you the cut you want, change stylists.

Another common fear is asking for a certain hairstyle and leaving the salon with another. To prevent this problem, don't describe the style at all—bring a picture with you. Cut one from a magazine or draw it for the stylist. This way there should be no mistaking the style you want.

Regarding a new hair color, many women are afraid they'll leave the salon with a completely wrong color. Make sure your hair colorist pays special attention to your skin tone and eye color. Help her out by wearing a minimum of makeup for the first appointment so she can see your skin undertones. Avoid making a drastic color change all at once, change it gradually so others will notice you look better—brighter—without really knowing why.

When going to a salon for a permanent, many women fear getting a perm that is too "tight." If this happens to you, try living with the perm for a few days to find out if you might like it. If you're still dissatisfied, go back to the salon. They should be able to relax the perm by pouring perm solution through the hair or using a heavy conditioner to weigh down the hair and flatten the curl.

Another way to reduce this problem is to make sure that you are getting an acid perm. An acid perm can be repermed tighter or looser as soon as one week later. An alkaline perm is irreversible and you'll have no choice but to let the perm grow out.

Never settle for second best from a hairstylist. Your hairstyle is a very personal thing. If you're not happy with the hair care you are receiving, change hairstylists.

A woman's hair has often been called her "crowning glory." As the child of the King, you are a princess. If your crown needs a little polishing, you've now got the information to help you go from drab to sparkling!

On the next few pages you'll see exciting photographs of women who have incorporated the ideas from this book. You too can be an attractive representative of the Lord Jesus Christ. Take a look at some of the wonderful changes that are possible.

With proper hairstyling and makeup, *you* can look great! To prove this, look at these "before" and "after" photos. The "before" pictures show average, everyday faces and unstyled hair. The "after" photos are truly sensational!

Here's how you can go from

With proper hairstyling and makeup, *you* can look great! To prove this, look at these "before" and "after" photos. The "before" pictures show average, everyday faces and unstyled hair. The "after" photos are truly sensational! Here's how you can go from

DULL TO **DYNAMITE!**

KATHY
Small eyes and mouth...needs softening colors that highlight eyes and proportion features.

DEANNA
Small eyes, round face, naturally curly hair...needs strong makeup and easy care hairstyle to lengthen face.

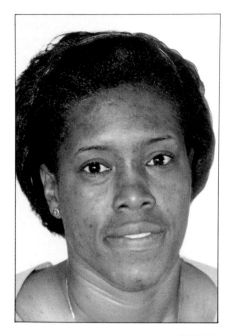

SARAH
Uneven skin tone, strong features...
needs lots of color to brighten face
and even out skin tone. Hair
now balances jawline.

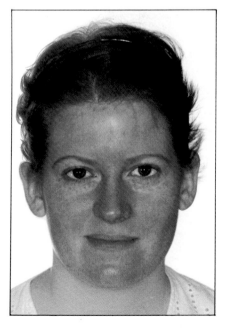

TERA
Delicate, pale skin, bland features...
needs definition of high-voltage blue
eyes and thick mane of hair.

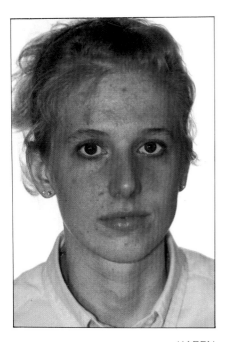

KAREN
Pale blonde, "too young" look...needs
strong makeup to enhance
super eyes and define cheekbones.

INEZ
Prominent features, intense coloring...
needs refining with lively, but
subdued makeup, highlighting and
softening cheekbones.

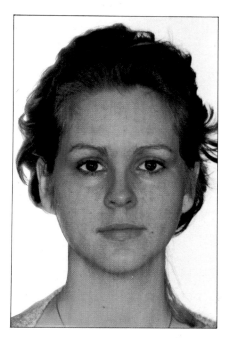

DEBBIE
Average, all-American face, eyebrows
need shaping...great with makeup
and new blonde streaks in hair!

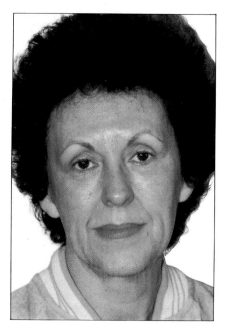

LEONA
Deep-set eyes, prominent brow...needs
shading to bring into proportion;
looks elegant with makeup.

Assignment

What changes would you like to make in your appearance at work? _____

What changes would you like to make in your appearance at home? _____

What do you feel you need to change in each of these areas?

Hair _____

Skin _____

Body Presence _____

Exercise _____

Clothing _____

Try to make these changes as soon as possible.

To pamper yourself (you deserve it!), check off the thing that you will do for yourself this week. Every week after this one, do one more thing listed below until you've checked off every item.

☐ Give yourself this homemade facial: Mix half an avocado, 2 tablespoons of lemon juice, and two crushed almonds. (Almonds should be raw and unsalted.) Apply to face. Relax for several minutes. Rinse with tepid water.

☐ If it has been more than six weeks since your last trim, make an appointment at a hair salon to have your hair trimmed. If you don't need a trim, make an appointment for a shampoo and set.

☐ Buy yourself a new scarf or pair of earrings—something you can use in coordinating your new wardrobe.

☐ Give your hands a thorough manicure—complete with softening hand lotion to help you in hand communication.

☐ Try one of the massage techniques in chapter 6. Enlist the help of your husband or best friend if you feel like it.

Every day remind yourself to use eye contact in your communication with others.

If you need them, buy: plain, white toilet paper
Ivory soap
underpants with a cotton crotch

PART THREE

The Confident

Woman Values

Her Relationships

Learn About:

- How to communicate effectively
- Unforgettable love gestures
- Spicing up your marriage relationship
- Lounge wear to help you look great at home
- Keeping romance alive
- How to handle sexual temptation
- Dealing with fear and guilt
- Changing fantasy into reality
- Forgiving yourself and others
- Forgetting the past

9
Communication:
Key to
Confidence

If I talk,
Will you hear?
If you hear,
Are you listening?
If you are listening,
Will you understand?
If you understand,
Will you care?

—author unknown

Have you ever tried to communicate with someone who doesn't seem to know what you are talking about? For some reason, you just can't "get through" to this person. This problem often leads to frustration and hurt feelings.

Too many have too little training or practice in the art and skill of communication. It's no wonder that one of the biggest problems facing a relationship is ineffective communication.

To communicate openly and effectively, you must be able to *express* what you are feeling and then you must be able to *listen* with empathy as the other person shares with you. A conversation always has two sides, and the other person must be willing to give and take as well. If either person is threatened or defensive then real communication will not take place.

In male/female relationships this is especially evident. Women and men are often far apart in emotional responses. For example, most men show love, caring, and intimacy through touch and sex. During an argument, a man may reach out and try to touch a woman. This may be his way of saying, "I care, I do love you, and this disagreement really isn't as important as it seems." Unfortunately, most women miss the point, tend to think the man is only interested in sex, and respond with, "You don't love me . . . you don't have any sensitivity."

The first step in communication is to get on the same wavelength. The other person needs to know how you really feel, and you've got to understand his or her point of view.

The best way to do this is to develop the use of the "I" language." This is a method of saying how you feel without causing any misunderstanding on another's part.

My grandson knows this language well. At three years old he says, "I'm hungry," "I love you," "I want a drink," "I want to go outside." I never have to ask myself, *Now what does he mean by that?* I always know exactly where I stand with him.

Before long, Aron will go off to school and he'll learn that he shouldn't say "I" when he begins a sentence. He'll learn to be tactful, sometimes untruthful, and at times, manipulative. Instead of saying, "I want to go shopping," he may say, "Wouldn't you like to go shopping, Grandma?"

Soon the awful truth will come, he will learn to communicate just like everyone else—vaguely.

To avoid this vagueness, begin to say "I" this or "I" that. Don't leave your meaning up in the air.

It is so easy to communicate vaguely. I find myself doing it when I'm making plans with my husband. Usually it happens when we try to decide where to eat lunch. It goes something like this:

> Jim: Where would you like to go for lunch, honey?
> Me: I don't know. Where would you like to go?
> Jim: Whatever you want is fine with me.
> Me: Well, I'd like to please you . . .

Three minutes later we're still where we started—tossing the question back and forth. It continues on like this:

> Jim *thinks:*   *I know she likes seafood.*
> Jim *says:*   How about the Fish Galley?
> I *think:*   *Pizza is his favorite.*
> I *say:*   What about pizza?
> Jim *thinks:*   *I had pizza for lunch yesterday, but if that's what she wants I'll go again.*
> Jim *says:*   Great, let's go.
> I *think:*   *I really don't want pizza because I'm trying to lose weight, but I'll go to make him happy.*

We end up going to a place that neither of us wanted to, but we were each trying to please the other. Once we sit down to the meal—

> Jim says: The pizza crust is too hard.
> I say: I only came here because you wanted to! Don't complain to me!
> Jim says: What? It was your idea to come here in the first place!

As you can see, communication breaks down because neither one of us said what we really meant. Our communication would have been clearer, simpler, and easier if we'd just used the "I" language and said what we really felt.

To avoid situations like this, memorize these five basic rules in communication:

1.   Say what you mean.
2.   Believe what you hear.
3.   Trust that you're both on the same side.
4.   Be clear.
5.   Listen carefully.

If you will begin to put these five rules into action, you'll find your communication skills improving. You'll have less time for arguments, fewer misunderstandings, and you may even develop a genuine rapport with others.

Don't use communication as a means to destroy someone. Try not to hurl accusations which only make people defensive. Instead, remember the "I" language.

For example, if you usually say, "You make me mad," "You're always criticizing me," or "You're never around," try saying, "I feel mad," "I feel I can never please you," or, "I feel a need to have you around."

Using "I" language is not selfish or arrogant. It is simply the best way to communicate. To me, it *is* selfish to second-guess or blame someone else by using "you" language.

Starting your sentences with the word you can often sound accusatory. In the same way, starting your sentence with we can include others who don't necessarily agree. For example, "We would love to go to the movies with you tonight." (Maybe the other person wouldn't!)

Try to avoid saying "Let's . . ." as it can incorporate the other person without consulting them. Instead say, "I would like to do such and such, would you?"

Be careful that you don't disguise "you" language like this: "I think you . . ." This is just camouflaging the accusatory tone!

For good communication don't use absolute statements such as, "That is an ugly painting," or "That is the prettiest dress you have." Whenever possible, substitute "That is . . ." with "I prefer," "I like," or "I dislike." If you impose your ideas on someone else through absolute statements you risk offending, insulting, and alienating them.

Although I endorse "I" language as the clearest and best way to communicate, I want to add one caution. *No matter how honest you are, try not to blurt everything out without regard to how your words will affect another person.* Use common sense and loving feelings to help guide you.

To turn conversation into real communication, you will also need to develop other good habits.

To begin with, don't interrupt someone who is conversing. Even if they are telling a story with mild inaccuracies, resist the urge to correct them. Does it really matter if the story is a little mixed up? Nothing will insult or belittle a person more than your interference.

Second, be careful not to heckle people by looking upward in exasperation or making gestures behind their backs as they talk. If you really need to set the record straight, do it at another time or later on that day.

Don't give away confidential or embarrassing information about others without getting their permission. They may not want anyone else to know what they paid for a new car or whether they are wearing a wig. Do you want them telling everyone how much you weigh or how much money you make?

I was at a seminar once when a man got up to introduce his wife. It was a nice introduction until his last statement. He said, "Oh, and you may have noticed that she has a different color of hair than she did last year." At that point you can be sure everyone looked to see what color her hair was now. The woman was very embarrassed and had to come to the platform and give a speech after that!

Remember, some information should be kept confidential.

Not too long ago, my husband and I were late for an appointment and as we walked in the door I said, "Jim couldn't find his keys, that's why we're late." I immediately put the blame on Jim, when instead I should have just apologized for being late. It is not always necessary to make excuses, especially at the risk of someone else's feelings. Blaming someone is a sure way to dead-end a conversation with them.

In the same way, you should be careful about telling funny stories at another person's expense. Fight the impulse to tell everyone about the time you were trying to dock the boat and the other person tripped and fell into the water. It might be an amusing story, but unless you have the other person's permission, you may be risking a friendship. Try not to do anything to belittle anyone else.

If someone begins to tell a joke or story that you have heard a hundred times before, resist the impulse to roll your eyes, groan out loud, and make snoring noises! Instead, try to listen attentively. It won't hurt you to listen to it another time, but it may hurt the speaker if you ridicule him.

Just so you don't make the same mistake, always ask the other person, "Have I told you this before?" This will solve problems all the way around.

Finally, don't interpret what another person is saying, with phrases such as, "What Bob means is . . . ," Bob will probably resent your interruption and may not even agree with your interpretation.

In all your conversations, be thoughtful of others. Let them know you care by showing respect for their ideas.

Conversation Starters

The most difficult thing in conversation is to come up with the first sentence. The second most difficult thing is to keep the conversation going once it begins. With a little practice you can become a good conversationalist even with people you've never met before. Here are some helpful hints to make conversation a breeze.

Begin with friendly comments, not too personal but not stiff or just polite. Simplicity is the key. Some of the best openings are:

1. Hi (or hello). My name is _____. What's yours?
2. How are you doing? (Ask this sincerely and be prepared to listen to the answer.)
3. May I sit here and talk with you awhile?
4. I feel embarrassed, but I'd like to meet you!
5. That's a nice sweater (or shirt, etc.).
6. Excuse me, I don't think we've ever been introduced.

You can also begin a conversation with anything you feel the other person and you have in common. It can be a mutual friend or a song that is playing.

To keep a conversation moving, try these suggestions:

1. Ask questions. The questions should promote more conversation, such as, "Where are you from?" To continue the conversation you might ask, "Did you enjoy living there? What did you do when you were growing up there?"
2. Talk positively. Conversation should make the other person feel good. Say something pleasant and use his or her name. For example, "Barbara, I understand you work for Dow Industries, what is it like?"
3. Watch your body language! Remember to lean toward the person. Never cross your arms against your chest. Nod your head with interest, and don't look all around the room as if you are bored with the other person.
4. Listen to what the other person is saying and be receptive to conversation "jewels" that may be dropped. If the other person says she enjoys warm weather, ask if she has ever been to Hawaii or other warm climates. If she has, pursue the subject of what she did there, and so on. If she hasn't, ask where she would like to go if she had a chance, what she would do there, and so on.

You will probably have an easier time communicating with someone if you are perceptive to what that person is saying. Do you feel you have a strong sense of woman's intuition? Can you interpret what others may be saying non-verbally? Take this simple quiz and find out!

Check the box nearest the statement that best describes you. It doesn't have to be exact, but choose the one you identify with most strongly.

1. I enjoy working with things rather than working with people. □ □ I love helping others and would like to be a social worker, teacher, or counselor.
2. As a leader, I am concerned with getting others to work together. □ □ As a leader, I'm concerned with getting the job done.

3. I would rather be popular with many people than have just a few close friends. ☐ ☐ A small group of intimate friends is more important to me than a lot of acquaintances.

4. Children should obey their parents—period. ☐ ☐ Children should be allowed a vote in matters that pertain to them.

5. Museums bore me, and I'm not inclined toward artistic endeavors. ☐ ☐ I like to think that I'm artistic, and I love going to museums.

Perceptive people generally have these characteristics: a genuine liking for people, a concern for getting the job done, a few intimate friends, a respect for children, and artistic inclinations.

For each check you have in the left column, add 1 point, for each check you have in the right column, add 5 points. The higher your score, the more perceptive you are. If your score is 20 or above, you are very perceptive and probably have an easier time communicating.

If your score is 13 or below, you may want to pay closer attention to body language and nonverbal messages. Communication may be more difficult for you, but it is still possible!

Communication is more than just conversation. Conversation is important to everyday living, but communication is essential to loving relationships. Without some solid communication skills, your intimate relationships won't stand a chance.

Here are some important ways to develop loving communication:

1. Look into the eyes of the people you are talking with and ask them to look directly at you when you speak.
2. Ask other people what they are feeling.
3. Remember those feelings when you talk.
4. Ask people to clarify what they mean if you have any doubt.
5. Repeat what you understand the person to mean.
6. Ask whether you both really mean the same thing.
7. Find out if you have enough information to really understand, if not, get more information.
8. Are you confused about what you understand the other person to mean?
9. If so, explain that you are confused and get it cleared up.
10. When you exchange your thoughts, the result is happy communication. Express this happiness to the other person.
11. If the conversation causes hurt and pain, relate your feelings and share how you would like things to be different.

If you still have problems communicating and the relationship is not open and happy, it may be best to admit a need to seek professional counseling. This may be the only way to restore the relationship.

In communication, it is imperative that you express your love to the other person. This can work miracles in healing broken relationships. Don't be afraid to let someone know you care.

I'm reminded of my grandson when he was just learning to talk. I flew to Modesto, California, to visit him, and as I stepped out of the airplane he came running to me saying, "Gwa Gwa Jo! Gwa Gwa Jo! I wuv you!" I knelt down to greet him, and we hugged as tightly as possible, oblivious to the rushed and annoyed passengers who moved around us.

I had had a busy weekend and when he said, "I love you," the words warmed my heart, eased the stress, and helped to heal my weary bones. It was precious to me, and I've often thought back to that moment and the spontaneous way Aron shared his love with me.

It makes me wonder how many times I could show more spontaneous love, excitement, and verbal affection when I get off the airplane to see my husband. Or even the times he comes home after a busy day at work.

How about you?

Unforgettable Love Gestures

There are many fun and creative ways that you can show others you love them. It can even be exciting to make these plans with certain people in mind. It gives you a chance to really study their personalities and interests.

I know of one woman who sent a "thank you" to a friend by way of a spice cake with the words *thank you* written in frosting on the top. The receiver loved spice cake and had even asked for my friend's recipe.

Another woman fixed a picnic basket for two and sent it to her husband's office. When he discovered the basket he also found a note tucked inside which said, "Meet you at the office at 4:00 o'clock—let's go on a picnic." That was one day her husband didn't stay too long at the office—he was ready to go at 3:45!

For my daughter's sixteenth birthday party, Jim and I wanted to do something special. We "kidnapped" her (blindfold and all) and took her to her favorite place—the ocean. We had invited three of her closest friends and her boyfriend and had rented a condominium to stay in for the weekend. It was a complete surprise to her and is still her favorite birthday party!

You too can think of unforgettable ways to let someone know you care. It doesn't necessarily have to cost anything, except maybe a little time and effort. Possibly it could be as simple as writing your husband a love letter and slipping it under his pillow. Maybe the new mother in your church needs a baby-sitter for an evening and you could volunteer.

Whatever it is, do something unforgettable for someone you love this week. Plan something special at least once a month and let others know you care. You'll be pleasantly surprised at what it will do for you as well.

Touching

I could never write a chapter on communication without including a vital part of communication—touch. Researchers have found that we all have "skin hunger." This is the undeniable desire to be lovingly touched—whether through a hug, backrub, or even simply holding hands.

If you love someone, you need to be communicating with him or her through touch. It can be the tool that breaks down the barriers between you and another person.

In my seminars I come in contact with women from all over the country. In talking with them I've come to realize how important touch really is. So many women have expressed to me their need for physical contact. Not just sexual contact, but loving, physical communication. It is so wonderful to be able to hug, wrestle, and touch wholesomely.

Recently I received this letter from a girl. She wrote:

Joanne,
Thank you so much for reaching out to me last night—for holding my hand for a few seconds. I can't quite explain or even completely understand, but I am awed by you and your kindness, grace of manner, and the warmth of your touch. I am encouraged in simply knowing you . . . I am grateful for your influence in my life!

You may never know when your simple act of reaching out to hold another person's hand will change his or her life. A smile, eye contact, and a touch can reach a soul. *Never take your love for granted,* let others know by reaching out to them.

I can't help but think again of my newly adopted Korean granddaughter, Kimmi. For her, touch has been literally lifesaving. Coming from Korea at the age of two and a half she didn't know how to hug or kiss. Although she was a happy child she was also withdrawn and aloof. She was on the way to becoming a disturbed child and a bitter adult. Loving touch helped to change the course of her life. Today you can't meet her without getting a great big smile and an even bigger hug. After being physically starved for affection, she now bestows it freely on everyone she comes in contact with. She has been a real inspiration to me and has taught me a new meaning to the phrase, "Hold on for dear life."

True communication can be risky. It can be frightening or elating. But, it is always worth it. Life is too short to waste on misunderstandings and fears. In your communication with others, keep in mind 2 Timothy 1:7, "For the Holy Spirit, God's gift, does not want you to be afraid of people, but to be wise and strong, and to love them and enjoy being with them."

Communication is an art, a skill, and a gift. Communication is also LOVE. Let this love flow through you to others today.

10

Marriage, Sex, and a Beautiful You

At eleven o'clock on a weekday morning in early summer, I was at the Pacific Ocean with a man. We stood with our arms around each other as we admired the marvel of the sea against the peace of the blue sky. Suddenly a woman jogged past us and shouted, "I know who you are—but your secret is safe with me!"

Immediately we jumped apart—then we laughed. "What made us jump like that?" Jim asked, "After all, we're married to each other!"

"I guess we feel guilty because we're having fun when we're supposed to be working," I said.

Although we had started the day with every intention of working, that all changed when Jim phoned me from the office and said, "Summer is here. I'll meet you at the ocean in an hour."

I was working hard to finish a book and was already at our beach house, but I've come to learn that when my husband says, "Summer's here," I'm in for a treat. I was out of the house and headed to meet Jim within the hour.

We did so many of our favorite things—walked on the beach, tossed a Frisbee, looked for sea animals, and combed the beach for agates. It was as romantic as any movie.

Then we kissed good-bye and got into separate cars. As Jim returned to the office and I went back to our beach house, I felt renewed and lighthearted. The best thing about having a rendezvous with your husband is that you can enjoy all of the pleasure and have none of the guilt!

As I think about that time at the ocean, I realize that it had all the ingredients that make love affairs so appealing. It was romantic, impulsive, and deliciously luxurious.

For a few brief hours we were able to be carefree and self-indulgent. Those hours represented an idealized fantasy—one that most men and women desire.

This self-indulgent time is often missing from a marriage. This lack of romance and spontaneity can contribute to a stale marriage. Love affairs are usually fresh, new, and exciting. Marriages are too often stagnant, old, and boring.

It's so easy to become entrenched in the struggles of daily life. Sometimes your problems can seem insurmountable. Stress can drain your energy.

If you feel this way, take a few hours or a weekend to refresh yourself and your marriage. Do something you've always wanted to do. Surprise your husband and renew some of that romantic spark.

The next time I'm overcome by the daily pressures of work, you can be sure I won't hesitate to say yes to another walk on the beach.

It is important to make time for each other regardless of mundane time stealers such as grocery shopping, children's school appointments, traffic jams, and household chores. You may need to reschedule your daily responsibilities so that one parent isn't overburdened with ''at home'' responsibilities. This is especially true for working women. If both partners work, home responsibilities should be shared.

Here are some exciting ways to help you make time for each other:

1. For an occasional weekend, hire a baby-sitter to take the children out of the house for several hours. The minute they leave, forget whatever else you're doing and focus on each other. Do something you've been wanting to do for a long time. Enjoy this uninterrupted time of being together.
2. If your children are older and can be left in the house without you constantly watching them, tell them that you and your husband need time alone. Set an alarm clock to ring in one hour. Let the children know that when the alarm rings you will come out of your room. Then retreat to your room and do not allow the children to interrupt.
3. Try to do household chores together. Try cooking or grocery shopping together. This will provide you with the time to get caught up on what has been happening in each other's lives. You'll probably have a good time too!
4. Without the children, check into a motel for a weekend. Allow yourself the luxury of going where you want, eating where you want, and sleeping late in the morning. If baby-sitting is a problem, exchange the weekend with another couple who have children. That way you can baby-sit for them when they want to get away for a weekend too.

It's not easy to be a wife, parent, and businesswoman. Sometimes work seems all important and relationships get shuttled off to the wayside. It is important to take time to enjoy your husband—don't take your time together lightly. Whether you've been married a few months or sixty years it is never too late to begin implementing these creative ideas. Just make sure it's not a one-shot deal—consistently plan special activities. You'll not only improve your relationship, you'll improve your life.

My husband and I have now been married over twenty-six years and I can honestly say that I love him more now than ever.

Because this book could never be written without his support, I want you to meet him. Here's a photograph of Jim and me taken right around the time of our twenty-fifth wedding anniversary.

For our twenty-fifth wedding anniversary, our two children, Deanna and Bob, planned a wonderful celebration.

Deanna wrote this lovely poem for us:

> How different you both are . . .
>   Jim—A laughing child of August,
>   Summertime blue,
>   Silent strength,
>   A practical heart.
>
>   Joanne—September's eager child
>   Autumn's fire,
>   Crackling enthusiasm,
>   A romantic heart.
>
> As different you two as summer and fall,
>   Yet when weighed on love's scale,
> You balance one another just as
>   seasons balance out the year.

Jim and I renewed our vows to each other and our pastor Don Bubna shared with us some thought-provoking insights about marriage. What he had to say was so pertinent to me that I want to share it with you.

Every marriage is a statement of what *you* believe about marriage. Your twenty-fifth wedding celebration is significant because it is your statement about staying together. I know that both you and Jim have different temperaments . . . I hope you don't feel sad about this. That's the gift of most couples I know. In marriage we are different from one another and because of this we may not always get along.

The basis of a humanistic marriage is "I love you and I know I love you because I *feel* like it and if next year I do not feel like it, then I will leave you."

Christian marriage is based on commitment. It is not dependent on how you *feel*. Love is action. Love is doing.

In the thirteenth chapter of 1 Corinthians, the Apostle Paul reminds the church that they are to resolve their conflicts and their differences by loving one another. He does not define love so much as he describes it. Paul says, "Love suffers long . . . love is not for the short run, it is for the long run. It is kind . . . that's how you know when love is being displayed. Love envieth not, it wanteth not itself, is not puffed up, does not behave itself unseemingly, seeketh not its own, is not easily provoked, thinketh no evil, and does not imagine bad things about another, only good.

Love does not rejoice in evil—doesn't say "AHA! I knew it would be that way." Love rejoices in the truth. Love bears all things, believes all things, endures all things, and hopes all things.

At that anniversary celebration, Jim and I exchanged renewed commitments and verbally appreciated each other's parts in our lives. You may need to do this with your husband, no matter how long you've been married. To show you what I mean, here is what Jim and I said to each other that night:

Joanne: Twenty-five years ago tonight I told you that I would love you, honor you, and live with you for the rest of my life. Tonight I do love you, honor you, and I want to live with you the rest of my life.

I also want you to know what makes me really love you. The first thing is that you are very strong mentally, emotionally, and spiritually. In many ways you are much stronger than me.

You are very tolerant and you meet my emotional needs which gives me peace and contentment in our relationship. You are very steady and I can't really remember seeing you in a bad mood.

You are humorous, laugh easily, are industrious, and a hard worker. You're generous, unselfish, and caring—not only about the big things, but about the little things as well.

I have never doubted your love for me. You are a man of integrity and I trust you implicitly. You've also done more to help develop and establish my self-esteem than anybody else I've known.

I thank God for you and your life and that He has given me the gift of you, my husband.

Jim: As I look back over the last twenty-five years we've spent together, I know there have been times of stress and there have been difficult times. But, the overwhelming times of joy that we have had, make me forget all those brief times of stress and difficulty.

I thank the Lord for giving you to me and for the love that we share. Thank you for loving me and accepting me as I am. Thank you for being the mother that you have been to our children. You have set a wonderful example to them and you have made them believe in themselves.

Your enthusiastic and exciting spirit has brightened and enlivened my days. I love and admire you for the way that you have dedicated yourself to the call that the Lord has given you and for your steadfastness and desire to help others become all they can be. I pledge to you my continued love and support. I eagerly look forward to the next twenty-five years with you!

Marriage will be what you make it. Some women cry for a separate identity. However, when two people are happily married, their lives become so intertwined that they cannot have a totally separate existence. No one really lives his life alone. Through others, and especially those we love deeply, we can find ourselves.

There are many forms and varying degrees of commitment in marriage. It is based on what each couple determine their life together ought to be.

Remember, you can only work on *yourself* in a marriage. You can't change the other person, they have to change themselves.

The key to understanding a successful marriage is to realize that each partner thinks of the other person first. This promotes a willingness to work at a relationship.

If you want to be a confident woman, one who is more outgoing and mature, what better place to start than with your marriage relationship?

A marriage contract does not limit a couple's growth. Instead, it suggests that you are mature enough to share your life through good times and bad, sickness and health. This means *change*.

One of the major changes that occurs when you get married is that sex suddenly becomes "legal." For many women this creates problems of its own.

During my seminars the women are given the chance to share some of their needs. One woman said, "I have been praying for several months about a problem my husband and I are having. I need to open myself up sexually to my darling husband. I love him so much."

Another woman said, "Pray that I will desire intercourse with my husband and have him know that I enjoy it. I want to satisfy him, and he wants it to be as fulfilling for me as it is for him."

It is my consensus that many, many women do not have a satisfying sex life. Some of them blame it on themselves; most of them blame it on their husbands. Possibly, both parties are to blame. If you are struggling with this area in your marriage ask yourself these simple questions. It will help you determine any areas that you may need to change.

1. Do you know what excites your husband?
2. Have you ever tried to find out what excites him?
3. Does your bedroom look inviting and exciting?
4. Do you avoid going to bed with curlers in your hair or oily creams on your face?
5. Are you warm and affectionate to him during the day?
6. Do you let him know what excites you sexually?
7. Have you ever asked your husband if he is really pleased with you sexually?
8. Have you ever asked your husband what he would like to change about your sexual habits?

9.   Do you give yourself freely to your husband?
10.   Do you wear becoming nightgowns? (Not just flannel!)
11.   Are you willing to make love at unorthodox times?
12.   Do you ever initiate sex?
13.   Do you ever leave love notes in his lunch box or under his pillow?
14.   Do you send love notes to him at his work?
15.   Have you prayed with him about an improved sex life?

You should be able to answer at least thirteen of these questions with a positive answer. If you can't, you may need to work on the areas that you answered negatively.

Lovemaking is something that women should enjoy—not just endure. In the "dark ages" (not so long ago!), women were taught that sex was a duty. Sexual enjoyment was for the "loose woman," not for the lady.

Today, women are finally beginning to realize that sex is a vital part of the married woman's life. The act of lovemaking is not only a source of intense bodily pleasure, but it can also help make a woman beautiful all over.

Have you ever heard the story about the ugly duckling who got married and turned into a beautiful, graceful swan? That story is not just a fairy tale. Sexual pleasure not only boosts your spirit, it benefits your body as well.

If you doubt that God intended women to enjoy lovemaking within the bounds of marriage, read Song of Solomon. It is loaded with mutual sexual pleasure.

You may also want to think about this: Women were created with a clitoris. The clitoris has only one purpose—to receive and transmit sexual pleasure. If a woman were not to be sexually fulfilled, God could easily have eliminated that otherwise unnecessary part of a woman's anatomy.

To help you realize the potential in your sexual pleasure, it is necessary to dispel a few myths.

The first myth is that good sex is common and natural. On the contrary, good sex is neither common nor natural. It is something that needs to be learned and fostered. You've got to work at a good sexual relationship.

Second, there is the worldly myth that sex is best when it is illicit, and when it includes many and varied partners. For most people this is simply not true. Erotic satisfaction is usually the result of time, familiarity, and again, effort, and cooperation.

The third myth is that single people have more and better sex than married people. Quite frankly, the opposite is true. Married couples on an average are much more satisfied and enthusiastic about their sex lives than single people. Marriage brings the commitment that is so vital to a fulfilling sex life. After all, lovemaking is the total opening of yourself to another person. That kind of vulnerability brings risks which are minimized in a loving, committed relationship.

If you feel that you are unfulfilled in your lovemaking, I would recommend to you Clifford and Joyce Penner's book, *The Gift of Sex* (Word Books, 1981). It can give you some other practical guidelines to becoming the fulfilled woman God intends you to be.

In our society today we are constantly being told we should be instantly gratified. We are also told that passion should last forever—and if it doesn't, we ought to get out of the relationship and find another partner.

I believe this false philosophy is encouraging the divorce rate and also promoting the idea of romantic divorce. By definition, passion is short-lived. To expect it to last forever is unrealistic. However, the trust, loyalty, commitment, and appreciation that accompany a marriage, usually lead to greater sexual fulfillment which overshadows passion.

Susan was the last woman anyone in her social circle would have thought wanted a divorce. At forty-five, Susan seemed to have everything going for her. She had a good business, a lovely new home, a handsome husband in his late forties, two children who were both in college and doing well. Susan's life was the envy of her friends, but she herself felt dissatisfied. She felt that something was missing and she wanted fresh excitement.

By the time her husband realized what was happening, it was almost too late. Susan had found another man. She thought she was really in love with him. He was so attentive. She worked with him and he seemed to make her feel years younger. He didn't push or pull her or make demands. Sex with him was exciting and new. He was carefree, fun-loving, and easygoing; and she thought she wanted to be with him all the time.

Susan's husband persuaded her to go for counseling before they dissolved their marriage, and she began to see that her extramarital relationship was not really love at all. It was actually an escape from a marriage that had become routine and unfulfilling.

Through counseling (many sessions), Susan began to see her husband as the unique personality she had once loved. They discovered they were still in love with each other although it was buried beneath resentment and insecurity. They chose to revitalize their marriage and today are happily discovering each other all over again.

It takes a lot of work to say, "Okay, let's renew our lives," but the effort, though great, is well worth it.

Some of my single friends, although they enjoy their single status, have shared that they feel the absence of a committed partner. The comment I hear most often is, "I miss not having somebody to come home to at night, someone to share the events of the day with."

This is the essential ingredient of a successful marriage—constant, dependable emotional support and positive affirmation.

If you refuse to work out the conflicts in your marriage (and we all have conflicts), you are running away from reality. Turning to another partner is not the solution. If you keep running, you will be doomed to a lifetime of unsuccessful relationships.

It is time to get rid of your romantic illusions about marriage. Romance doesn't have to go, but your illusions do. I'll be covering this in more detail in the next few chapters.

Again, I want to emphasize the importance of nourishing your commitment.

It is so important to identify with your partner, allow him to evolve and change, just as you also need the chance to "grow."

If you are unhappy in your marriage, you may need to develop some of your interests. My friend Barbara was disenchanted with her marriage and her life. Instead of seeking a new relationship, she chose to change herself. She worked on open communication with her husband and also became involved in an oil painting class, something she'd dreamed of doing for years.

Satisfying some of her interests made her less dependent on her husband for every need, and her marriage relationship blossomed. Her husband is proud and supportive of her endeavors, and she feels more complete as well.

You may also need to keep verbally saying, "I love you." I know this has been covered elsewhere in the book, but it is important enough to be restated here.

I know a woman who has been married over thirty years and for twenty of those years she had not told her husband that she loved him. They are Christian people, and everyone in the church thought they were the perfect couple.

After attending one of my seminars she learned about the importance of saying, "I love you." That night she went home and decided to try it.

Just as they were about to go to sleep, she quietly whispered, "Honey, I love you." Her husband did not respond. Then she noticed that his side of the bed was shaking and a man who never cried was weeping openly.

When he gained his composure he said, "You have no idea how long I've waited to hear you say that. It has been many long, lonely years."

She has since written to me that they are now on their second, third, and fourth honeymoons. They are verbally expressing love to each other, and it has restored their relationship.

Do you need to tell your husband you love him? Don't let any more time go by. Do it right now. Call him at work, write him a note, do it however you can.

It is also urgent that you say, "Thank you," to your spouse. Even the little things that he does should be verbally appreciated by saying, "Thank you."

Write down the things you are thankful for in your spouse.

Now write down the things he does *daily* for which you are thankful.

Next time you see him, show him what you have written. Then remember to say, "Thank you," on a daily basis—even for the small chores or errands he does.

You can also show your appreciation in other ways. One man confided in me that the one reason his marriage failed was lack of appreciation. His wife always nagged him about not showing her he cared, so one evening he came home with a dozen roses. There was no special occasion, he just wanted to say, "I love you." Instead of thanking him, his wife asked, "How much did they cost?" He said, "Twenty-five dollars." She blew up and said, "Twenty-five dollars! That would buy a lot of groceries. How could you do that?"

The man had not failed to provide money for groceries and he was extremely hurt by her attitude. Her failure to appreciate his gesture left him feeling unloved and rejected. He felt she didn't value his judgment. They are now divorced.

If your husband brings home a gift, show your appreciation and love. If your husband wants to take you out to dinner, even if you think you can't afford it, go anyway. Let him be responsible to see that the bill is paid. Once in a while your finances can take second place to your love relationship, right? Of course, you've got to use common sense—don't blow your whole budget on one evening of entertainment!

Maybe you feel that showing appreciation isn't your problem—you wish your husband would bring home a gift, *anything,* so you could appreciate it! If you feel this way, ask yourself what you are doing to encourage gift giving and dinners out. What are you doing to build a love relationship? It's never too late to start. Remember though, love and appreciation habits cannot be acquired instantly, they require time and patience.

To encourage a love relationship, try touching your man as often as possible. When you are together, even if you're doing household chores, try to touch him in passing. It can be a caress on the shoulder, holding hands while you watch television, a passing hug, anything to keep touch alive.

Do you remember what it was like when you were first dating and going together? You probably couldn't keep your hands off each other.

Start doing this again and soon it will become second nature to you. As I practice this, I find that I can quietly take my husband's hand while sitting in church, or I can slip my arm into his when we stand to sing a hymn.

Touch never becomes meaningless because it is such a vital need all humans have. Touch will only increase your love relationship.

I believe that a good-bye kiss in the morning should *never* be forgotten. It shouldn't be done perfunctorily, but it shouldn't be ignored either. It is so easy to get engrossed in everyday tasks and let little gestures become unimportant.

There are times when I am so busy with my work that when Jim comes into the house I barely look up or say hello. What a difference it makes when I enthusiastically greet him with a kiss. I need to keep in mind how lucky I am to have a husband who comes home to me!

Besides touching more, what else did you do when you were first dating? Nothing is better for your relationship than going out and doing some of the things you did before you were married. Was there a certain place you loved to go to? Did you have a favorite activity to do together? Even though it may seem hard to get away, make arrangements to do it anyway.

A friend of mine regularly thinks of something she would like to do with her husband that they haven't done in a while or have never done before. She writes her ideas down on a piece of paper and then shows it to her husband. She then suggests that they act out exactly what is on the paper. For example, the other evening she wrote, ''Bruce and I are driving through the countryside, sitting close together, my head on his shoulder. We drive past a quaint country inn and decide to stop for lunch. After a delightful lunch, we decide to take a leisurely stroll through a country meadow. We talk and share about our dreams for the future. We sit down on the grass and he kisses me tenderly. . . .''

Write your own idea of a romantic day with your husband:

_____

_____

_____

_____

_____

_____

_____

Why not plan to do it soon?

I've noticed something curious about married women. It seems that often they let their appearance deteriorate after the wedding ceremony. It is important to keep up your physical appearance. When you were dating you took time to look good, be well-groomed, and wear attractive clothing. It is almost more crucial to do these things after marriage. After all, it is unfair to your spouse if he thought he knew you and you turn out to be different. It can also threaten your relationship.

One woman who attended my seminar wrote, ''Please pray for me. My husband and I are very close to separating. He is flirting with a friend of mine. He says there's nothing wrong with it, even if it hurts me. I'm overweight and he's tired of it. I have trouble liking myself.''

Looking good at home doesn't mean that you have to be uncomfortable. There are so many lounge gowns and leisure clothes that are very attractive. Here are some examples of leisure and lounge wear for the woman who wants to look good at home.

These outfits are modeled by Liz Lundmark and her daughter, Dawn. Liz is an Image Improvement teacher in Lake Oswego, Oregon, and Dawn is her assistant. The clothes are provided courtesy of Intimique.

If you'd like, you can even make your own lounge wear. Look for a pattern in your favorite fabric store, or try this simple, quick, and inexpensive idea for making a lounge gown without a pattern.

Start by choosing a pretty, washable fabric. You'll need 3 yards of 45-inch-wide material. If you are under 5 feet 2 inches tall, buy a little less than 3 yards; if you're over 5 feet 8 inches tall, buy a little more than 3 yards.

When you get the material home, fold the fabric in half so that you still have a 45-inch width, but the length is now 1½ yards. You should be holding two thicknesses of fabric (see illustration 1).

(Illus. 1)
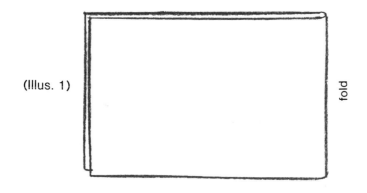
fold

Fold the material in half again, this time keeping the 1½-yard length, but half the 45-inch width. There should be a fold along the side and along the bottom (see illustration 2).

(Illus. 2)
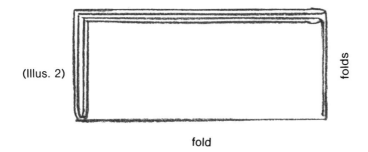
folds

fold

Where the four folds meet, cut a small part out of the corner (see illustration 3). This makes the neck opening.

(Illus. 3)

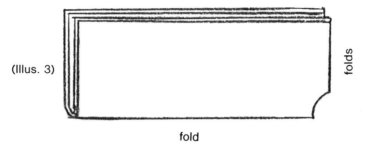

folds

fold

Open up the fabric and cut down from neckline on one side of the fabric about 4 inches. This will allow you to get the gown over your head (see illustration 4).

Sew the two side seams, keeping the wrong sides of the material together. Sew the seams as far up as you want, leaving room for the armhole openings. Always start your side seams from the hem up, don't close in the space for your arms!

(Illus. 4)

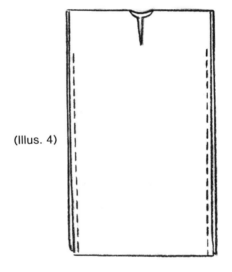

Finish hem, neckline, and armhole openings with iron-on, fusable hemming tape or hem by hand. Add a snap closure to neck back opening. Wear the garment loose and flowing or belt it and accessorize it all you want! (See below.)

Options: Finish neckline with lace or a matching fabric collar. Use your imagination!

Along with looking good at home, you may also need to work on controlling your temper. Mistreatment of your mate through an explosive temper is one of the fastest ways to break up a relationship. If you have a problem with your temper you may want to try this suggestion.

Imagine that Jesus Christ is watching every move you make. (In a sense He is, but imagine that He is actually in the same room with you—not in spirit but in person!) Instead of letting it all out, you may find you'll check your responses before you let go. In time, this will become a habit.

Of course, there may be times when your temper gets away from you. If it does, make sure you sincerely apologize. Say, "I'm sorry, will you forgive me?" Asking the question, "Will you forgive me?" demands a response. Just saying, "I'm sorry," does not. It is better to get a response from the other person so that you will know where you stand.

Finally, here is a questionnaire to find out whether you are spending "grade A" time with your spouse. This is time that is spent giving him your full attention with no distractions.

1. Do you ever go out for an evening of bowling or "fun" together?
2. Do you ever go out for a romantic evening dining together?
3. Do you ever eat by candlelight at home together?
4. Do you ever go on picnics together?
5. Do you really have fun, laugh-filled times together?
6. Do you avoid spending your weekends baking or doing the wash while he works on the car?
7. Do you have long discussions about your dreams and your relationship?
8. Do you do things (outside of household responsibilities) just for the two of you?
9. Do you surprise each other with little gifts?
10. Do you try to get away, at least once a year, to a new place where you can be alone together?

For each question you answered "yes," score 2 points. For each question you answered "sometimes," score 1 point. For each question you answered "never," score 0 points.

If your score is below 15, you need to improve your grade-A time together. You may be in a rut and need to improve your relationship little by little.

Even though our dreams about the "perfect marriage" are often shattered, most people hope that the partner they choose will last them a lifetime. As our society continues to put a premium on impersonal, mechanical marriages, the bond of intimacy becomes strained.

However, marriage is still the single greatest adventure two people can begin and endure together. I hope you're now on the way to making it the best relationship it can possibly be.

The confident woman values her relationships . . . and love relationships most of all.

11

Temptation: The Unmentionable Sin

Lisa first began to suspect something was wrong when she found herself making excuses to be with him. Her thoughts turned to him every minute of the day. It became harder and harder to concentrate on anything else and she lived for the next time she'd see him.

Lisa was not a teenager experiencing her first crush. She was thirty-three years old, a Christian wife and mother. She was sexually attracted to someone other than her husband.

She knew she shouldn't feel that way but was unprepared for the onslaught of her emotions. She loved her husband but felt overwhelmed by this attraction to another man.

No one had ever told her that a wedding ring doesn't insulate you from sexual temptation. She believed that Christian women were supposed to be immune to such problems.

Ministers seldom preach on it, Christian books seldom discuss it, and Christian couples almost never acknowledge it—even to themselves.

I remember the first time I learned that my husband thought another woman was attractive. I was literally devastated and I ran out of the house, hid behind the side of our garage, and cried my eyes out.

I felt miserable, worthless, alone, and rejected. Looking back I realize how ridiculous it was. Jim wasn't confessing an affair, he was just acknowledging a simple fact: Men find women attractive and vice versa!

However, there are many Christian women, like Lisa, who have either experienced this sexual attraction mentally or acted on it physically and don't know how to handle it.

159

I know this is true because I've heard this problem repeated in many of the prayer requests I receive. Here is just a sampling of what the women have to say:

- I'm having another man's child, not my husband's. I ask for forgiveness. I love this child very much.
- I was a pastor's wife for thirteen years—three years ago my husband left me, divorced me, and married another woman. I am so lonely and feel that lack of human love. I know God loves me, but I feel the need for human love.
- My husband is a Christian, but has deep bitterness toward me because of an affair I had several years ago.
- I desperately need to pray that the Lord will help me forgive my husband for having an affair. He claims for the fourth time that the relationship is over. I want to believe him if he is truthful.
- My husband and I are separated. He wants to come back. I'm a Christian, he isn't. Affairs have been involved in both our pasts—abortion in mine.

As you can see, Lisa is not alone. In fact, I would venture to say the rarity is the woman who has not experienced attraction to a man other than her husband.

If this is true, why do we still cloak this temptation in awful secrecy? Why is it still so taboo?

The answer may lie in the fact that as Christians we are often taught our bodies are sinful. We mistakenly believe that sexuality is a result of man's fallen nature.

This is simply not true. Genesis 1:27 says, "So God created man in his own image, in the image of God created he him; male and female created he them" (KJV).

We were created as male *and* female. We were not created in God's image *in spite of* our bodies, but rather *as* bodies. Sexuality is not an afterthought to the creation of mankind, instead it is an essential part—something to rejoice in!

Your sexuality is an integral part of who you are. This is something to be thankful for, not something to be ashamed of.

However, Galatians 5:19 does say, "But when you follow your own wrong inclinations your lives will produce these evil results: impure thoughts, eagerness for lustful pleasure."

So, we know that we are inherently sexual beings, and now we also know that our own sinful nature can pervert the natural sex drive into sin.

How can you know which is which? When is attraction a temptation and when does it become a sin? If you're a married woman and feel that you may be attracted to someone other than your husband, here are some danger signals to look out for:

1. Are your thoughts straying to daydreams about you and the other man?
2. Do you wish that you could actually carry your daydreams out?
3. Do you intentionally do things to get his attention?
4. Do you create situations to be alone with him?
5. Are you reading the Bible less frequently?

6. Do you wonder what everyone else's "secret sin" is?
7. Has your family taken on a lower priority for you because of him?
8. Do you feel confused, mixed-up, and uncertain about him?
9. Do you find yourself behaving differently around this man? Walking or dressing suggestively?
10. Do you find yourself eagerly looking forward to the next time you'll see him?

If you can answer yes to any of these questions, then you are heading down a dangerous path. Yielding to mental adultery could very easily lead to physical adultery—and yielding to either kind of adultery carries with it some extremely high costs.

Anita was one woman who thought she would never face sexual temptation. For years she was a devoted wife and mother. Most of her activities revolved around her church and there she just didn't have much conversation with the opposite sex.

When her youngest child went to college, Anita went back to work. At her new job, she worked daily with a thoroughly fascinating man. She felt herself being drawn to him. She still loved her husband and didn't want to act on her feelings, but found them difficult to control.

Through persistent prayer she was finally able to gain control of her emotions, still work with the man, and remain faithful to her husband.

Her husband never knew about the temptation and still does not. Anita felt she couldn't tell him, her mother, her pastor's wife, or even her best friend. She felt she would have been rejected if her "secret sin" were known to anyone else.

Happily, Anita solved her problem alone. Lisa's story, however, did not end as happily.

Lisa found herself living with a husband who was too busy to really listen. At church she found a Christian man who would.

It all began innocently as she and this other man laughed, shared, and prayed together. He seemed to understand her so much better than her husband did.

Although this man was also married, he and Lisa found ways to be together. As they discovered more and more things they enjoyed about each other, they felt a need to discuss their feelings for each other.

Once this happened, it was a short step to "holy" kisses and warm embraces. Finally, the sexual tension increased to a point where they felt it impossible to hold back. Their affair was consummated physically.

Months went by and they snatched opportunities to be together. It was romantic and thrilling—but also guilt-ridden, stressful, and ultimately disastrous.

Lisa discovered she was pregnant with the other man's child. This resulted in a confrontation with her husband and a divorce followed. The other man also got a divorce and he and Lisa were married.

The marriage lasted less than a year and Lisa is now struggling to raise her children alone. She says, "I had no one I could turn to . . . not one friend or church member. I felt totally alone and didn't know how to handle my sexual attraction. I wish I'd never given in to mental and then physical adultery. I know my life would be different today if I hadn't.''

These two stories ended quite differently, but they have one thing in common—both women felt isolated by their sexual feelings. They both felt it could not be discussed with anyone.

Instead of ignorance and denial, these women needed sound guidelines for dealing with the temptation. Remember, temptation itself is not a sin, yielding to the temptation is and only God can give you the strength and power to fight it.

The first step in giving up misguided affection is to see the other man less frequently. Stop doing any special favors for him, make conversation with him only in public places, and don't allow yourself to be alone with him. If it is impossible for you to avoid being alone with him because of a work situation, you should consider changing jobs or at least departments. You've got to break your former patterns of association with him. Continuing to seek his company will only make the temptation stronger.

Second, you need to admit your feelings of temptation and find out the depth of the temptation. Some Christians have misunderstood Matthew 5:28 which says, ''But now I tell you: anyone who looks at a woman and wants to possess her is guilty of committing adultery with her in his heart'' (TEV). I don't believe this means that a glance at a member of the opposite sex is equivalent to adultery. But, it is mental adultery if you are captivated by the thoughts and emotions that accompany it. If you are continually thinking along the lines of adultery, it is a serious problem.

If you know your thoughts or actions are adulterous, you need to ask God's forgiveness. This may be difficult as for some reason we find it hard to ask forgiveness for sexual sin. We can readily admit feelings of anger, impatience, lying, and gossip, but sexual sin seems ''worse.'' Please realize that God does not list sins in order of importance! There are no better or worse sins. To God, sin is sin—*period*. And guess what else? Your sins have already been covered by the blood of Jesus. There are no qualifications for forgiveness, all you've got to do is ask for it.

Forgiveness is essential to any sin, but especially to sexual sin, as further problems can arise if it is not dealt with. Guilt and depression are common problems associated with sexual sin. Don't let them come between you and God's forgiveness. You may need to learn how to release your guilt about your sexual feelings. If forgiveness is an area you struggle with, you'll find more help in the last chapter of this book.

In addition to this, you may also need to share your problem with a Christian friend or counselor. This can be very helpful, but I must caution you to choose your confidant wisely. Many people may not be able to understand or hold your confidence, even though they are basically trustworthy. DO NOT discuss your problem with the man involved—or any other male friend.

If you do tell a friend, ask her to pray with and for you. Also ask her to continually confront you and make you accountable for your actions until the temptation is resolved. Be very honest with her. Don't tell her the problem is resolved if it really isn't—this will do you no good.

If you have already yielded to the affair and know it must stop, take the risk of praying, "Lord do anything You have to do to make me willing to stop." Then be prepared for the Lord to work. You may not like the methods He uses, but they will ultimately be for your benefit.

Be careful about confessing your problem to your spouse. For some women it has been an answer and for some it has been disastrous. This matter should be handled with extreme care, prayer, and counseling. If you feel you must make a confession, go to a Christian counselor first. Tell him or her about it. Possibly that will be the only confession you'll have to make, as not every husband is able to handle this situation with grace. Although you may *feel* better by getting it off your chest, it can cause irreparable damage to your marriage and may harm innocent children.

You should, however, seek to renew your love relationship with your spouse. Chapter 10 can give you some valuable information on how to go about doing this. The main problem may be in seeing your husband as the man you first fell in love with.

Pastor Ted Zabel of the Christian and Missionary Alliance Church in Salem, Oregon, once shared this thought with Deanna. She went to him for premarital counseling and this is what he said: "When you've been married awhile you may find that your husband only meets 95 percent of your needs. There may come a time when you meet someone who satisfies that other 5 percent. It will be tempting to exchange your 95 percent for the 5 percent that seems so vital. Don't ever do this. Five percent is never worth exchanging for 95 percent!"

Verbalize all the things that you first loved about your husband. They are still there, even if they are buried. Work on putting romance back into your relationship with him.

You may also need to renew and honor your commitment to God and His plans for your life. Spend time letting Jesus Christ put His finger on your past hurts and emotional needs—let Him wrap His healing arms around you.

Use prayer *daily* (even minute by minute if necessary) during this temptation time. Reaffirm your trust in God and seek His will and direction for your life. If the Holy Spirit is controlling you, your deepest desire will be to obey God. *Allow* the Holy Spirit to control you.

God is able to meet your emotional and physical needs—not just your spiritual ones. Spend quiet time alone with Him. Read His Word!

Since you can't cut the other man entirely out of your life, ask God to purify your thoughts and desires about him. Allow God to channel the emotions you feel into areas of service to Him.

Ultimate victory over sin comes from your dependency on the Holy Spirit. Rely upon Him for the strength to become all God intends you to be.

Memorize Galatians 5:24 which says, "Those who belong to Christ have nailed their natural evil desires to his cross and crucified them there."

Depriving yourself of personal pleasures will bring greater rewards in the future. Believe that God is shaping you from an eternal point of view. Guard against living on a "feelings" level. Temporary satisfaction should not be exchanged for eternal values. When wrong thoughts come into your mind, thank the Holy Spirit for pointing out the temptation then "replace" the thoughts with those toward your husband. Build him up in your mind.

Finally, associate yourself with people who are committed to spiritual growth and Bible study. If you are not involved in a vital Bible Study, join one. You may want to find one that is just for women if you would feel freer in this type of group. Whatever you decide, choose a group that is growing and alive. It is essential that you realize fulfillment in God's ways, not in your own desires.

In closing, I want to share a poem that was written by a woman who wrestled with the very temptation I've been discussing. She is now on the other side of an affair and she knows the guilt that can obsess your mind. Possibly, her poem will be of help and inspiration to you as you deal with this problem.

> The struggle of the soul,
> The tearing and churning of the mind,
> The frontline combat in the emotions—
> > Essentially, my will against God's will.
>
> A part of me doesn't want to give up this sin.
> My flesh cries out to be satisfied,
> To rush in my own way,
> > Thwarting God's perfect plan for me.
>
> It's a tooth-and-nail fight
> To kill this flesh in me,
> To deny my screaming emotions,
> > To follow the hard, narrow path.
>
> It causes a cold, subtle oppression
> Waving over my whole self,
> Blocking my heart's joy,
> > Making effort of a smile.
>
> But, intermittently I see the overview—
> I can catch a glimpse of God's purpose for this temptation
> And my growth from it.
> > I am passing more of the tests designed for me!
>
> The school of the Spirit
> Keeps invading the soul's struggle,
> Calming my mind and instructing my emotions.
> > Eventually, God's will wins.

12

Fear, Fantasy, and Guilt— Destroyers of Confidence

I will never forget the day my younger child went off to college. Tears welled up in my eyes and the sobs came uncontrollably. My "little Bobby" was leaving home to attend college three thousand miles away.

I just knew that I would never see him again. I just knew he couldn't survive that far away from home. I just knew it was going to be a disaster.

Why? Why was I so unrealistic about his departure? Because I was frightened. I was frightened of losing him and I was frightened of the future.

My fears made me miserable and what was worse, they were unrealistic fears. My son was ready for independence and deep down I knew he was capable of taking care of himself.

Bob went off to college at the Massachusetts Institute of Technology in Cambridge and believe it or not, I actually saw him again! In fact, he graduated from M.I.T. after four years and is now working in the United Kingdom. As I look back, I realize how foolish I was in my unrealistic fears.

I had another lesson in the fear department when I visited Bob while he was in college. He lived in a co-ed dormitory and again I felt frightened. I wasn't sure whether a co-ed dormitory was the best place for a Christian young man. However, I felt a little reassured when I realized the male and female students had separate rooms—the rooms were just in the same building!

While I was in his dormitory I used the women's restroom. As I entered the stall, I noticed the walls had graffiti all over them. Usually I don't care to read graffiti, but one wall caught my attention. On it, the women from Bob's dorm had written a list of the attributes of the men who also lived in the dorm.

Much to my surprise, I noticed that under *Sexiest Eyes* several men were listed, including Bob Wallace. Reading further, I found out that the *Sexiest Legs* category also included Bob Wallace.

At this point, I was beginning to wonder if some of my fears were realistic after all! Maybe I hadn't prayed hard enough for my son! What kind of impression was he making?

Then my eyes fell to the last category which said, *Nicest to Bring Home to Mom.* The only one listed was my son, with these comments: "Bob Wallace— good Christians always impress Mom."

My fears were relieved. I thanked God that my son displayed a witness even in an atmosphere that most would call counterproductive. All that day I glowed, knowing that my son was having an impact on the people he knew.

What would have happened if I'd only read the first two lists and then gotten all upset and stormed out of the bathroom? I would have felt fear and anxiety for no reason. Oh, I would have thought my fears were realistic, but in actuality, my son was doing fine.

What are the fears you have today? Are they realistic or unrealistic?

Realistic fears have a basis in reality. For example, a fear of falling when you're standing on the edge of a high cliff is realistic. There is a very real possibility that you could fall, and your fear serves as a reminder to step back onto safer ground.

If, however, you are fearful of "someday" falling off a cliff when in fact you live on flat prairie land, your fear is unrealistic.

Unrealistic fear is deadly. It poisons the mind and undermines your self-esteem. You cannot be a truly confident woman if you are fearful. In fact, you cannot be an effective Christian if you're fearful.

Let's take a look at the two main areas of unrealistic fear, how these fears can cripple you, and what you should do about them.

Uncertainty About the Future

The first and most common unrealistic fear is a fear of the future. This fear tells you that life is just going to be one big stress after another. What with the "economic times," your "health problems," and your "insecure relationships," the future is just bound to be horrible.

What kind of life can you live today with that kind of future ahead of you? Fear of the future produces worry. It has been said of worry that it "does not empty tomorrow of its troubles, but robs it of its strength." Worry does not solve or subtract from your problems; it actually multiplies them!

The responsibilities of life are not meant to be heavy burdens, but rather opportunities to fulfill purpose in your life.

How much of your worrying is actually realistic? Here's a rough approximation of what most people worry about:

Things that never happen	40%
Things in the past that can't be changed by all the worry in the world	30%
Petty worries	10%
Needless health worries	12%
Real, legitimate worries	8%

Maybe you need to realize, as Mark Twain so wisely said, "I am an old man and have known my troubles, but most of them never happened."

Don't let fear of the future destroy today. God is saying to you, "Life is to be lived, I have a purpose for you *today.*"

What do you fear today? Write it down:

_____

_____

_____

Isaiah 41:10 says, "Fear not, for I am with you. Do not be dismayed. I am your God. I will strengthen you; I will help you; I will uphold you with my victorious right hand."

From this verse, what three things does God say He will do for you?

_____

_____

Claim this verse! When fear begins to creep into your life, remember that God has promised you His strength, His help, and His support.

Fear is not of God. If you are fearful, in effect you are saying, "God, I doubt Your love and wisdom for me." Nothing could be further from the truth. God's love and wisdom are perfect.

Trust and believe God *today.*

Fear of Failure

The worst kind of fear comes from a sense of personal failure. This type of fear says, "If only . . ."

"If only I'd known I'd get laid off from my job . . ."

"If only I'd been smarter . . ."

"If only my spouse had been more supportive . . ."

"If only I went to a good church . . ."

"If only I'd been born to different parents . . ."

This fear searches for someone else to blame. Since personal failure is hard to accept, it is easier to believe it is someone else's fault.

When this happens we often lash out at the person we are blaming. This leads to anger and resentment and the problem multiplies.

As resentment builds, we fall into depression and begin to wonder if life is worth living. The result of fear can make life look very dismal. However, there is one very important point you must understand: *GOD IS FAR MORE AC-COUNTABLE FOR YOU THAN YOU CAN EVER BE TO HIM.*

God has made Himself accountable to you. Did you know that God has made over eight thousand promises to you through the Bible? And God *cannot* break a promise.

So, it is not what you are or what you do, but rather, WHO HE IS and WHAT HE DOES AND WILL DO.

Psalm 23 beautifully reminds us of God's accountability. Read it through carefully and underline the words *he* and *you* every time you see them. Keep in mind that God cannot fail you and what He says is true.

> Because the Lord is my Shepherd I have everything I need! He lets me rest in the meadow grass and leads me beside the quiet streams. He restores my failing health. He helps me do what honors him the most.
> Even when walking through the dark valley of death I will not be afraid, for you are close beside me, guarding, guiding all the way.
> You provide delicious food for me in the presence of my enemies. You have welcomed me as your guest; blessings overflow!
> Your goodness and unfailing kindness shall be with me all of my life, and afterwards I will live with you forever in your home.

Just as you should not blame others for your own mistakes, you should not blame *yourself* for *another's mistake.*

During a recent seminar a woman shared this prayer request with me, ''I am a pastor's wife, a trained beauty consultant. I can do all of the right things on the outside, but because of several mishaps in my life—i.e., molested at age four, raped by our youth leader at twelve . . . inside I ache desperately. I am at present being treated for severe depression.''

This woman suffers from depression because of someone else's sin. Her sense of failure is a result of another person's problem. If you have a problem with this type of personal failure, I urge you to seek professional counseling.

If you believe yourself to be worthless because of someone else's abuse, you are believing a lie. Satan is the father of lies and he wants you to believe them, but Jesus Christ wants you to break out of your bondage into the freedom of His truth. We hear lies all around us. Many of us grow up believing them. Here are some lies believed by many people:

- Correction is rejection.
- I cannot accept what I don't understand.
- If I am wrong, that means the other person is right.
- If you love me, you'll let me have my own way.
- Being hurt is the worst thing in the world.
- Peace at any price is good.

What lies are you believing today?

Ask God to break the chains of the lies you are believing. Jesus Christ promises us that His Holy Spirit will lead us into all truth. John 8:32 says, "you will know the truth, and the truth will set you free."

Fantasy

At one point in the early years of my marriage I can remember driving long distances (over three hours) in our car without once talking to my husband. I lived in a fantasy world. I could not accept myself and found it easier to make up my own world. I would retreat into this world for long periods of time. Possibly you know what I am talking about. Fantasy can be one of the most destructive games around.

Fantasy is an ability to create, within your mind, an *unreal* world. Fantasy is not constructive use of your imagination, it is the destructive means of escaping reality.

Fantasy does not help you to cope with the real world, only to escape from it. It is important to understand that fantasy is different from *hope*. Hope, combined with prayer, leads toward certainty—fantasy does not.

Fantasy is also different from goal setting, planning, and dreaming of future success. Goal setting means working *toward,* it means action. Fantasy is an inability to act within reality.

Before I understood this, I used to pray, *Lord, don't make me give up my fantasy world. I want to live in a world where everything is wonderful. I want to run things my own way and I can do this in my fantasies.*

It came to the point where I was spending hours a day just fantasizing. I was bored with housework, caring for my small children, and the humdrum of everyday responsibilities.

I fantasized about a world where life was exciting and I was pampered and secure. This fantasy involved every area of my life and only served to make me miserable.

I felt more and more depressed with my "real" circumstances and because of this, I allowed temptation and then sin to enter my life. Finally I had to come to the place where I said, "Lord, I *don't* make a better God than YOU. Please take control of my life again."

God is the God of the real world, but He can also be Lord of your fantasy world as well. If you'll let Him, Jesus Christ can help you begin to realize positive dreams and aspirations for your life.

Don't waste any more time fantasizing about "might have beens." The only thing stopping you from reaching your goal is *getting started* and *never quitting.*

What ideas do you have in your mind today? What would you like to do with your life? Do you want to start an exercise program? Start a new business? Join a new church? Read the Bible more often? Whatever it is, don't waste it! Begin to do something about it today.

What is your idea?

_____

_____

_____

_____

Now begin to work toward making this goal happen. Your decision today will become tomorrow's reality.

Remember 2 Corinthians 6:2 (RSV) which says, "Behold now is the acceptable time; behold now is the day of salvation."

Start and never quit. Let God be Lord in your life today.

Guilt

Yes, guilt is real. However, it may not always be realistic. In this way, it is closely related to fear and fantasy.

According to many Christian counselors and the women I come in contact with during my seminars, over 30 percent of all appeals for help involve guilt-related problems. Only problems related to various fears rate higher.

Guilt brings with it a sense of inadequacy. This inadequacy in turn, undermines confidence. You can't become a confident woman by carrying around a load of guilt.

There are basically two kinds of guilt that we know as Christians. The first type of guilt comes from God. It is realistic and justifiable guilt. It is guilt over some sin in your life that hasn't been dealt with yet. The best response to this kind of guilt is to confess your sin and ask to be forgiven. This frees you from realistic guilt.

The second type of guilt comes from Satan. It is unrealistic guilt. Satan delights in and encourages this type of guilt. It is guilt that persists even though God has forgiven you. Satan uses this guilt to lie to you; to tell you that your sin has made you a failure and you are now incapable of success.

Satan wants you to dwell in the past, feel depressed, self-conscious, and worthless. He wants you to look *back* so that your *present* experience with the Lord is devastated.

If you continue to dwell in the past, you'll fail in the present. I see this illustrated for me at every seminar I lead. Women all over the country are sharing concerns like these:

- I need to learn to feel free from guilt in my life. I seem to feel guilty about so many things . . . past sins, guilt from not doing enough for others, etc. I am a Christian and I know God loves and forgives me . . . I can't forgive myself.
- I am struggling with my life . . . a great strife. I find what has happened to be very hard to forget and leave behind me. I love the Lord and know He will help me with this guilt, but I don't know what to do at times.

At one time, I, too, felt overcome by guilt. I literally wished I could die. Since I knew it was wrong for me to kill myself, I used to pray that the Lord would have me "accidentally" killed. Just like fear and fantasy, guilt made me want to escape reality.

If you are feeling unrealistic guilt, it is important to recognize it as a problem. Unrealistic guilt is not from God.

Let's take a look at 1 Timothy 1:16. Paul says, "But God had mercy on me so that Christ Jesus could use me as an example to show everyone how patient he is with even the worst sinners, so that others will realize that they, too, can have everlasting life."

Paul considered himself the "worst sinner," but he also realized God's complete forgiveness. He did not dwell on his past mistakes, but used them as an example of God's love and mercy.

God can use your past experiences as an example of His goodness to you. Don't let your guilt keep you from developing normally. You cannot be spiritually healthy if you harbor feelings of guilt.

The key is in truly believing God's unconditional forgiveness. This means being able to forgive yourself. Let's continue with this in the next chapter.

13
Forgiveness

A few weeks ago I was scheduled to give a seminar in a small town in Kansas. On route there, I was grounded in the Denver airport by fog on the ground in Kansas. There was no way I could make it to the seminar in time for my opening session that night.

My first thoughts were to despair; to question God's plan for that night. I felt heartsick as I called the church and let them know I was stuck in Denver and couldn't make it. It seemed that I was really letting the church down—even though it was beyond my control.

Although I was able to get to the seminar the following day and we had extralong sessions to make up for the delay, I still doubted God's wisdom.

Just a few days ago I received a letter that showed me how wrong I was to question God's plans.

The woman in charge of booking the seminar wrote to tell me that although I was unable to get to the Friday night session, the women in the church planned a special program anyway.

During this meeting, two sisters were reunited after struggling with jealousy and bitterness and two other women had their bitter relationship healed.

I am now so thankful that God planned fog! He knew that forgiveness and the healing of broken relationships were essential for that night.

Forgiveness is the most powerful force in the world. Remember when I said love was the most powerful force? I'm not contradicting myself. Love and forgiveness are the same thing.

Forgiveness is the language of love. Real love, at its deepest level, means forgiveness. This is the kind of love/forgiveness Christ has for you. Romans 5:8 says, ". . . While we were yet sinners, Christ died for us" (KJV).

God loved us even when He had no reason to—while we were still sinners! This is the essence of true forgiveness. This is God's unconditional love.

God's forgiveness is the first type of forgiveness you must experience. Without it, real forgiveness is not possible. You see, only God can truly forgive.

When God forgives, He forgets. This is the beauty of His forgiveness. As Corrie ten Boom said, "God throws our sins into the deepest sea and then posts a sign, 'No fishing allowed' " (see Micah 7:19).

God never goes fishing for your past sins and neither should you. God doesn't forgive you one day and then change His mind the next. God will never fling recriminations at you, He'll never make you feel guilty for confessed sin. He can't! Once He forgives you, He truly forgets it! God sets you free by His *total* forgiveness.

When I think of this, I always remember Psalms 32:1, 2 where it says, "What happiness for those whose guilt has been forgiven! What joys when sins are covered over! What relief for those who have confessed their sins and God has cleared their record."

It also says in Psalms 130:3, 4, "Lord, if you keep in mind our sins then who can ever get an answer to his prayers? But you forgive! What an awesome thing this is!"

God *has* cleared your record. Can you fully trust God for this forgiveness?

Trusting God often means believing totally, without evidence other than His Word. It has nothing to do with whether you "feel" forgiven. It has everything to do with realizing that God cannot lie. If He says you are forgiven—YOU ARE!

Think about how life changing this thought is. Now write down the way you would complete this sentence:

God forgives me; because of this, I can _____

_____

_____

Accept God's forgiveness and allow it to enlarge your appreciation of who God is. God's forgiveness is unmerited, unconditional, and unchangeable! What a God!

The second area of forgiveness is in forgiving others. If you are carrying a grudge against someone, you need to forgive that person. If you have been mistreated or abused by someone, it is imperative that you forgive. Failure to forgive others is more detrimental to yourself than to them. An unforgiving spirit is ripe for resentment, hate, and bitterness—all qualities that spoil your life.

During my seminars, I hear from many women who need to forgive others.

Some of them say,

- For the past year I have been working through this whole area of the past—which was a period of sexual abuse. Much healing has come, but I still hurt so badly sometimes. I really need to feel loved and affirmed.
- Please pray I will have a forgiving heart to my husband because today he forgot our sixteenth wedding anniversary and I feel hurt.
- Please pray for the healing of bitterness in my marriage relationship.

Forgiving others may be a long process. But, it is essential that you let go of past hurts, jealousies, resentments, and hatreds. The Bible is very explicit about why you must forgive others. It's because:

Whatever a man sows, that he will also reap.

Galatians 6:7 NAS

The measure you give will be the measure you get, and still more will be given you

Mark 4:24 RSV

Your heavenly Father will forgive you if you forgive those who sin against you; but if you refuse to forgive them, he will not forgive you.

Matthew 6:14, 15

When you are praying, first forgive anyone you are holding a grudge against, so that your Father in heaven will forgive you your sins too.

Mark 11:25

There are a lot of resentments that can build up in the course of a lifetime—or even one day. The only way to live happily is to remove these resentments from your life. The only way to do this is to forgive.

It may seem hard to forgive someone because what they did "was just not right." If this is your problem, I would encourage you to remember how much God has forgiven you.

Loving forgiveness is not judgmental. It does not say, "I'll love you if you treat me well," or "I'll love you if you love me first." Instead, it says, "I'll love you *in spite of* your sins."

This type of love is from God. It is something that can and should be evident if you are allowing Jesus Christ to be Lord of your life. In yourself, forgiveness is not possible. However, through Christ, forgiveness is the *only* possibility.

Allow Christ to lovingly forgive through you today. Who in your life do you need to forgive? Write down where you need to experience forgiveness:

_____

_____

_____

_____

Now visualize that you are walking toward the person you need to forgive. In love, you tell of your past resentments and hurts. You then ask this person to forgive you for not forgiving him or her.

Imagine the warmth and love of this healing moment. Allow this feeling to permeate your soul. Now take positive steps toward making this vision a reality. Call or go see this person as soon as possible.

Remember how much God has forgiven you and allow this forgiveness to extend to others.

Finally, allow this forgiveness to overflow onto yourself. This is the third kind of forgiveness and for most people, it is the most difficult.

Recently, a woman shared this prayer request with me, "A few years ago I was a beautiful model . . . now I feel ugly, as I've taken drugs and my past has made me ugly. I want to begin anew."

Do you want to begin anew? The first step is forgetting the past. This does not mean that you cannot remember the past, but it means that you do not sit and mull over past memories and mistakes.

Instead, get busy and DO SOMETHING. Get your mind active and positive about today. Forgetting the past means pressing on and not allowing it to interfere with your present or future.

Even though you may believe God has forgiven you, it is easy to be torn by guilt and remorse. "Why did I do it?" and "If I'd only known better!" are common self-reproaches.

Remember this self-reproach is a tool of Satan. When you begin to feel incriminated by the past, stop! Take a moment and say, "Yes, I made a mistake. But, thanks be to God, it is forgiven and now I can hear Christ saying, 'Let's get going!' "

Don't allow the past to frustrate the present so that you can't move ahead with God. Be careful about "classifying" sins. It is sad, but in the Christian church today, many sins are classified according to degrees of importance. There are certain sins that are "okay" and are forgiveable and then there are other sins that mark you for the rest of your life and you can never "get on with God." This is a complete misunderstanding of the Word of God.

Yes, there are sins that affect people's lives in more serious ways, but on the other hand, if you turn from that sin, Jesus says, "It's okay. My blood was shed so that you can be forgiven. You asked for it and you've got it! If you love me, get to work. We've got some things to get done."

You may need to learn the wise use of the wastebasket. By this, I mean you should be throwing out all the garbage in your life that is holding you back. Hebrews 12:1 says, ". . . Let us lay aside every weight, and the sin which doth so easily beset us . . ." (KJV).

Don't continue to carry around your past sins, temptations, prejudices, grievances, and worries. Dispose of them through the power of forgiveness.

The Apostle Paul learned the blessed use of the wastebasket in his own spiritual life. He said, ". . . Forgetting those things which are behind . . . I press toward the mark . . ." (Philippians 3:13, 14 KJV).

What a beautiful way to start every new day! Forget the things that God has already forgiven and press toward the things which He would have you achieve!

Assignment

Plan something special for someone you love. What would you like to do?

_____

_____

_____

_____

Now do it!

Is there someone you've met that you'd like to get to know better? If so, invite them to lunch this month. Use the ideas in chapter 9 to help you in conversation starters.

Within the next two weeks, plan a quiet, candlelight dinner at home with your man.

Set a goal to purchase or make a lounge wear outfit as soon as possible.

Closing
Thoughts

I'm hoping this book has given you some exciting ideas on how to become a confident woman. Now it's your turn. I urge you to invest your time and energy in the most valuable commodity in this world—YOU!

It is easy to dream dreams; not so easy to see them become reality. You may not yet be what you want to be, but you're already on your way if you are willing to *try*. Remember, no one ever "arrives," we are all in the process of growth. In fact, sometimes I feel I should post a warning sign that says, WATCH OUT! JOANNE UNDER CONSTRUCTION!

I'm so glad that because of Jesus Christ I don't have to do it all on my own. Neither do you! Ephesians 3:20 says, "Now glory be to God who by his mighty power at work within us is able to do far more than we would ever dare to ask or even dream of—infinitely beyond our highest prayers, desires, thoughts, or hopes."

Do your best and then *expect* great things to happen. Remember the old saying, "If you think you can, or if you think you can't, you're right!"

Lovingly,

Joanne Wallace

Index

Abuse, physical and mental, 36
Acceptance, 22
  self; 12, 17–18
Accessories, 50–51, 66
  belts, 51
  handbags, 50
  jewelry, 51
  scarves, 51
  shoes, 50
  shopping for, 66
Adornment, 19–22
Adultery, 159–64
Aerobic exercise, 93–94
Affirmation
  in marriage, 147
Aggressiveness, 29
Animation, 73
Anxiety. *See* Worry
Apology, 158
Appearance, 21–22, 37–38
  Christian attitude toward, 38

clothing style, 45–68
hair care, 119–28
improving, 37–38
marriage, importance in, 150–
  57
self-image, related to, 12, 37–
  38
skin care, 109–18
Appreciation, in marriage, 148–49
Arm massage, 107
Assertiveness, 29–30
Athletics. *See* Sports
Attitude, 18–19, 29–30, 34–35
Attractiveness, physical, 12, 20
  See also Appearance
Attraction, sexual, 159–64

Back
  exercise, 79
  massage, 107, 108
Barnard, Kathleen, 45

Beauty, 19–22
   See also Appearance; Attractive-
      ness, physical
Belts, 51
Bible study, 164
Biblical women, 20
Blame, 168
Blemishes, skin, 118
Blouses, 47–49, 53–56
Blowdrying, 124–26
Blush, 113–15
Body, 93, 108
   exercise, 93–104
   See also Health
Body language, 69–91
   positions and signals, 83–
      91
   space, 77
Boredom, 77, 88
Breast
   cancer, 104
   self-examination of, 105
Bustline, 96

Cancer
   examination of breast, 104–
      05
Capillaries, broken, 117
Career wardrobe, 52–56
Cause, working for, 37
Character qualities, 23–32
Cheek makeup, 113–15
Christlike attitude, 26
Christlike qualities, 23–24
Cleanser, skin, 109
Clothing
   accessories, 50–51
   colors, 48
   fabrics, 48
   life-style, 57–63
   personal style, 45–68
   shopping for, 64–68
   basic wardrobe, 47–51
   career wardrobe, 52–56
Color
   clothing, 48
   hair, 127
   makeup, 110–16
Commitment
   in marriage, 145, 147–48

Communication, 133–40
   body language, 69–91
   conversation, 135–39
   "I" language, 134–35
   loving, 138–40
   in male/female relationships,
      133–35
   nonverbal, 69–91
   perceptiveness in, 137–38
   rules of, 135
   touching in, 140
Comparison, 18–19
Compliments, 36–37
Confidant, 162
Confidence, 11–13, 17–22
Conversation
   and body space, 77
   for real communication, 135–39
   impressions made in, 73
   starters, 136–37
   use of hands in, 83
Cosmetics. *See* Makeup, Skin care
Counseling, professional, 36, 138,
      168
   marital, 147, 162–63

Decker, Bert, 80–82
Depression, 18, 36, 169
Determination, 28–30
Discipline, 31–32
Dresses, 47, 48
Dressing for day and evening,
      57–63
Dress With Style (Joanne Wallace),
      46, 109
Drummond, Henry, 26

Embarrassment, 27
Emotion, 36
Escapism. *See* Fantasy
Evans, Colleen Townsend, 18–19
Exercise, 93–104
   aerobic, 93–94
   flexibility, 78–79
   injury, 101
   "lazy day," 94–95
   for relief of menstrual cramps,
      101, 103
   stretching, 95–101
Exercise types, 102

Eye makeup, 111–12
Eyes
    as means of communication,
        74–76, 140
    circles under, 117
    patterns of expression, 75–76
    types, 111–12

Fabrics, 48
Face, 109–18
    makeup, 110–16
    shape, 113–15
    skin care, 109, 117–18
Facial, 129
Facial expression, 70–76
Failure, 167–68
Fantasy, 169–70
Fear, 27, 165–70
Femininity, 45–46
Flexibility, 78–79
Forgiveness
    God's, 162, 170, 171, 173–
        75
    of others, 175–76
    and sexual sin, 162
Foundation (makeup), 110
Frankl, Viktor, 37
Fruits
    of labor, 93
    of the Spirit, 24, 32
Fulfillment, 25–26
Future, fear of, 166–67

Gamma linolenic acid, 104
Gestures
    body, 83–91
    hand, 79–83
    of love, 139–40
Gift of Sex, The (Penner, Clifford
    and Joyce), 146
Gildersleeve, Jean, 22, 36
GLA. *See* Gamma linolenic acid
Goals, 29
God
    accountability of, 167–68
    in control of lives, 32, 169–70
    forgiveness from, 170, 171,
        173–75
    as foundation of self-worth, 19,
        34, 39

as help in time of temptation,
        162–64
    love from 22
    trusting in, 174
    See also Jesus Christ
Gracefulness, 78–79
Graham, Dr. John, 38
Growth
    in marriage, 145
    personal, 179
Guilt, 164, 170–71

Hair
    blowdrying, 125–26
    care, 124–28
    errors in styling, 120–24
    styling, 119–24, 127–28
Handbags, 50
Hands
    used for communication, 78,
        79–83
    holding, 140
Healing relationships, 138–39
Health, 93, 108
    breast examination, 104–05
    exercise for, 93–104
    menstrual cramps, 102
    muscle injuries, 101, 107–08
    premenstrual syndrome, 103–4
    vaginal infections, 106
Hip exercise, 97
Humanness, 32
Humor, sense of, 38–39

Identity, 45–46
    in marriage, 145
Illness, 93
Image of Loveliness, The (Joanne
    Wallace), 109
Impatience, 77
Inadequacy, 170
Injury, muscle, 101
Inner self, 12, 45–46
Involvement, 37

Jackets, 47–49
Jacuzzi, 101
Jesus Christ
    personal relationship with, 23–
        24

Jesus Christ (*cont.*)
   representing, 29
   See also God
Jewelry, 51
Joanne Wallace Collection, The, 109
Joy, 25–26

Kotler, Robert, M.D., 21–22

Laughter, 38–39
Leg massage, 107
Life-style, 12
   clothing as reflection of, 47–63
Lips, 115–16
Looks. *See* Facial expression, Outfits
Lounge wear, 150–57
   pattern, 155–57
Love, 24–25, 144
   expressing, 138–40, 148–49
   forgiving, 173–76
   gestures of, 139–40
   God's, 22
   need for, 12, 17, 24–25

Makeup, 109–18
   blush, 113–15
   cheek, 113–15
   color, 110–16
   eye, 111–12
   foundation, 110
   Joanne Wallace Collection, 109
   lip, 115–16
   rouge, 113–15
Marriage, 141–58
   appreciation in, 148–49
   Christian, 144
   commitment in, 145, 147–48
   conflict in, 147, 158
   counseling, 147, 162–63
   danger signals, 160–61
   expressing of love in, 148–49
   personal appearance in, 150–57
   renewal, 141–58
   romance in, 141–43
   sex in, 145–47
   temptation in, 159–64
   time together in, 141–43, 158
Mascara, 111–12
Massage, 106–08

Menstrual cramps, 102–04
Ministry, 18
Moisturizer (skin), 109
Mouth
   in facial expression, 73–74
   shape, 116
Muscles
   injury to, 95, 101
   massage of, 107–08

Negative thinking, 34–35
Notetaking, 77–78

Outfits
   basic wardrobe, 47–51, 52–56
   for different occasions, 57–63

Pants, 47–49
Past, 171
   and forgiveness, 174
Patience, 28–29
Pattern, loungewear, 155–57
Peace of mind, 26–27
Pelvic mobility exercise, 78–79
Penner, Clifford and Joyce (*The Gift of Sex*), 146
Perceptiveness, 137–38
Permanent, hair, 127–28
Personality, 23–32
Physical contact. *See* Touching.
Plastic surgery, 21–22, 38
PMS. *See* Premenstrual syndrome
Poem, 143, 164
Pores, enlarged, 117
Positions in body language, 83–90
Positive thinking, 34–35
Posture, 76–79
   exercises, 96
Potential, 23
Prayer, 163
Premenstrual syndrome, 103–04
Presence, 76–79
Pride, 20
Pulse rate, 94

Qualities, personal, 23–32

Rate Yourself Questionnaire, 39–41
Reality, 169–171

Recreation, 101–102
Relationships, 131–77
  illicit, 159–64
  male/female communication,
    133–35
  marital, 141–58
  with God, 23, 26
Renewal, marital, 141–58
Resentment, 175
Responsibility, 39
RICE (Rest, Ice, Compression, and
    Elevation), 101
Rouge, 113–15

Scarves, 51
Schuller, Robert, 19
Scripture
  Genesis
    1:27, 160
    2:23, 20
    12:14, 20
    24:16, 20
    29:17, 20
  Nehemiah
    8:10, 25
  Psalms
    1:3, 32
    23, 168
    32:1,2 174
    130:3,4, 174
    139:13, 14, 19
  Isaiah
    41:10, 167
    50:7, 28
  Jeremiah
    8:4, 27
  Micah
    7:19, 174
  Matthew
    5:28, 162
    6:14, 15, 175
    22:39, 17
  Mark
    4:24, 175
    11:25, 175
    12:31, 17
  John
    8:32, 169
    14:27, 26
    15:11, 25
    16:33, 26

Acts
  20:35, 37
Romans
  8:15, 39
  12:1, 93
  12.2, 39
1 Corinthians
  14:1, 24
  15:58, 28
  16:14, 24
2 Corinthians
  3:5, 34
  4:8,9, 29
  6:2, 170
Galatians
  5:19, 160
  5:22, 25
  5:22,23, 24
  5:24, 163
  6:4,5, 19
  6:7, 175
  6:9, 101
Ephesians
  3:20, 179
  4:15, 29
Philippians
  3:13, 14, 176
Colossians
  3:15, 26
  3:17, 29
1 Timothy
  1:16, 171
2 Timothy
  1:7, 27, 140
  2:1, 31
Hebrews
  12:1, 176
1 Peter
  3:3,4, 20
1 John
  4:16, 17, 24
Self-acceptance, 12, 17–18, 33–36,
    45–46
Self-control, 31–32
Self-esteem, 11–13, 168
  steps to, 33–41
Self-image, 11–13, 20, 22, 33, 35
Self-love, 17–18, 33
Self-rejection, 17–19, 22

Sex
    illicit, 159–64
    in marriage, 145–47
Sexuality, 160
Sexual temptation, 159–64
Shadow, eye, 111–12
Shampoo, 124
Shoes, 50
Shopping, clothes, 64–68
Sin, 159–64
Skin care, 109, 117–18, 129
    Joanne Wallace Collection, The,
       109
    makeup, 109–118
    problems, 117–18
Skirts, 47, 48
Smile, 73–74, 90
    as expression of love, 140
Song of Solomon, 146
Speaking. *See* Conversation
Sports activities, 102
Stomach exercise, 98
Stress relief, 106–08
Stretching exercises, 94–100
Style, clothing, 45–68
Suits, 52, 54–56
Sweaters, 47, 48

Talking. *See* Conversation
Temper, 158
Temptation
    danger signals, 160–61
    praying about, 162, 163
    sexual, 159–64
Thigh exercise, 100

Time together in marriage, 141–43,
    158
Touching
    as expression of love, 140
    as form of communication, 140
    in marriage, 149
Tops, 47–49, 53–56
Trust, 11, 174
Tummy exercise, 98
Twain, Mark, 167

Undereye circles, 117
Uniqueness, 18–19
University of Minnesota study, 12

Vaginal infections, 106
Vanity, 38

Waist exercise, 99
Walk, 78–79
Wallace, Joanne, *Dress With Style*,
    46
Wallace Joanne, *Image of Loveli-
    ness, The*, 109
Wardrobe, 46, 47–48
    basic, 47–51
    career, 52–56
Well-being, *See* Health
Women of the Bible, 20
Worry, 27, 166–67
    See also Fear
Wrinkles, 117

Zabel, Pastor Ted, 163

ORDER TODAY!!!

To order valuable services from Joanne Wallace, check the following areas of interest:

☐ Cassette albums on being a beautiful woman and success dressing.

☐ Please send me the free catalog of products available in *The Joanne Wallace Collection* of skin-care items.

☐ I'm interested in having Joanne Wallace come and speak in my area, please send me information.

                    ☐ Church group
                    ☐ Business group

☐ I'd like information on how I can become an Image Improvement Consultant.

☐ I'm interested in knowing more about how I can improve my image. Send me the name of an Image Improvement Consultant in my area.

My name is: _____

My address is: _____

City: _____ State: _____ Zip: _____

Home phone: (   ) _____ Work phone: (   ) _____

Mail now to:
         Image Improvement, Inc.
         P.O. Box 5162
         Salem, Oregon 97304
Or phone for more information: (503) 378-1969

ORDER TODAY!!!

To order valuable services from Joanne Wallace, check the following areas of interest:

☐   Cassette albums on being a beautiful woman and success dressing.

☐   Please send me the free catalog of products available in *The Joanne Wallace Collection* of skin-care items.

☐   I'm interested in having Joanne Wallace come and speak in my area, please send me information.

        ☐   Church group
        ☐   Business group

☐   I'd like information on how I can become an Image Improvement Consultant.

☐   I'm interested in knowing more about how I can improve my image. Send me the name of an Image Improvement Consultant in my area.

My name is: _____

My address is: _____

City: _____ State: _____ Zip: _____

Home phone: (　　) _____ Work phone: (　　) _____

Mail now to:
      Image Improvement, Inc.
      P.O. Box 5162
      Salem, Oregon 97304
Or phone for more information: (503) 378-1969